MONUMENT
FROM
THE KAISER

MONUMENT FROM THE KAISER

Years of Peace before WW1

Robert Von Hahnke

authorHOUSE®

AuthorHouse™
1663 Liberty Drive
Bloomington, IN 47403
www.authorhouse.com
Phone: 1-800-839-8640

Published by AuthorHouse   11/07/2012

ISBN: 978-1-4772-8975-4 (sc)
ISBN: 978-1-4772-8974-7 (hc)
ISBN: 978-1-4772-8973-0 (e)

Library of Congress Control Number: 2012921316

Introduction

I remember that as a young boy in suburban Detroit, I watched men going down to the end of the street every morning at the same time to catch the same bus to their jobs. They wore the same "uniform" every day and carried the same lunch box with probably the same type of food every day. I pictured them going to their jobs at a factory, putting part A on part B and joining the combination to part C for eight to ten hours every day. After a while one could predict the number of people at the bus stop, the color and style of their clothing, and the exact time when they would return. My father, although he took a car to work, fell into that same category. A suit (dark) with a tie (dark) every day, and he would go to Bray's on Michigan Avenue in Dearborn near the office for lunch almost every day. I fell into the same routine as a Detroit police officer. I was assigned to the school resource officer program and would begin each day with my partner, Bill Gillespie, stopping at the Rams Horn Restaurant for coffee and breakfast. After breakfast it was off to Cody High School to watch over the students and staff, making sure no one was killed or seriously injured during their day of education. I began to wonder what set us apart from the others who ended up at the same destination every day. Logic would dictate the path to our destination would set us apart from our peers. Part of that path is surely the background, even before our generation, that would bring us to who we are today.

I remember my father telling my brother Jim and me about the family history in Germany prior to World War I. It is very important to remember although a very large portion of the US population is of German descent, because we fought against Germany in two major wars, it was thought best at the time to not mention any personal history from Germany. I recall he told us of a Prussian military background and some of our relatives being high-ranking officers in the German army. That always sparked my curiosity. Was I the descendant of warriors or diplomats? Could my heritage have affected the way I look at things and reacted in certain circumstances? Who were these people the Von Hahnkes, and what did they do to set them apart from others?

At the time (1960s) I did what most people would do when researching an issue: I went to the library. I was in high school at the time and had a "study hall" period, which I usually spent in the library checking history books and periodicals for any evidence of the elusive Von Hahnke name. The search yielded no results beyond teaching a young man the virtue of patience, which would be useful many times later in life.

I did not give the matter much thought until the 1990s and the Internet boom. I was onboard in 1995 when the PC was making its way to becoming a necessary household item. I had just been divorced, and instead of sitting at home feeling sorry for myself, I took extension classes at the high school in Concord, New Hampshire, on the introduction to the PC. The computer opened up a whole new world of information at my fingertips, both locally and internationally. The search for the Von Hahnke name yielded no results, but like any medium, the PC can yield only what is sown. I patiently waited to see if the information would be posted and I could begin to harvest it.

Finally in 2003 I picked up a copy of *The Kaiser's Army* by Eric Dorn Brose and began to see the light of day. There were many issues citing a Field Marshall Wilhelm von Hahnke as a prominent figure in pre-World War I Germany. I was delighted to read a validation of the stories my father had told me long ago! This discovery fired the search for more factual information. I would periodically check the Internet to inquire if new information was available. The Internet for all of its glory is still basically like your savings account at the bank—you can take out only what is put in. The checking paid off in October 2004 when I found a picture posted of Kaiser Wilhelm II leaving the troopship *Rhein* after bidding farewell to German troops shipping out to China for the Boxer incident. The caption read, "Kaiser Wilhelm, General von Hahnke, and Prince Friedrich leave the troopship *Rhein*." At last I had proof positive of the family legend my father had passed on.

The gathering of information on relatives formerly living within the United States is very easy with the search engines available to everyone on the Internet. Looking for hereditary links from pre-World War II Germany, Japan, Poland, Russia, and some parts of China requires different tactics because of the destruction of records in those countries. My research led me on a different path—relying on newspaper articles of the period from locations not devastated by war. Although I am certain many of the news items would have been much more lengthy articles at the time in German newspapers, they were very small, but they were mentioned in newspapers in areas with large populations of those of German descent in the 1890s. I found many of the books written concerning that period surmise different parts of history. As a seasoned investigator I too will surmise certain issues based upon facts I have uncovered and give you the logical explanation for my conclusions.

Destruction can hit anywhere as I found in researching my father's military record. His records were destroyed in a fire at the Pentagon in 1967 by Vietnam war protesters. The army was able to come up with his dates of enlistment and discharge, rank at discharge, and nothing else. I had to rely on information he had passed on and pictures showing his service.

I continued my search, gathering information until I completed my quest with a trip to Odda, Norway, to investigate a 115-year-old family mystery, which included accusations of murder. The trip opened doors and solved the mystery that had been in the back of my mind for years. I found evidence beyond a doubt that my father's stories were true; and instead of being exaggerated, they were in fact grossly understated, possibly in an attempt at humility.

I chose the title Monument from Kaiser because the monument constructed in a neutral country came to symbolize the time of peace prior to the First World War.

I think it also represents the dedication of a fallen young navy officer's father to maintain peace during a very turbulent time in the world. There were many small wars during that period, and Germany managed to stay out of them. The Boer War involved Great Britain and the Boers of South Africa. The Boers were loosely of German heritage, so Germany could have used that as an excuse to enter the fray on their side, but it didn't. There was rumor that Germany was supplying the Boers with some arms, but that was never substantiated. There was also the Russian-Japanese War, which would have given Germany an opportunity to take advantage of a two-front war on Russia. That would have provided a golden opportunity to have the advantage over the larger Russian army, but that path was not taken. The kaiser chose to take the advice of his senior general and closest adviser, Wilhelm von Hahnke. Wilhelm von Hahnke was awarded prestigious medals from Russia and Great Britain, among other countries, for his peacekeeping efforts. I find it more than coincidental that within two years of General von Hahnke's death, the European countries were involved in World War I.

If nothing else, my search revealed there might be a pot of gold in your family history that you have no idea exists. I hope you enjoy the trip with me, especially the surprise ending. It shows you never can predict what you will find, but that makes the search worth it in the end. Take some time to find where you are from; you have the tools at your disposal, and what you find might just set you apart from the others waiting in line for the bus to work tomorrow—if nowhere else but in your own mind.

CHAPTER ONE

Detroit, Michigan, USA

Detroit, Michigan, in the late 1930s was both an exciting and a disappointing place to live. Its position between Lake St. Clair and Lake Erie gave it the advantage of economical water transportation of its products throughout the region. This also facilitated importing the raw materials necessary for production. The center of automobile production for the world, it was a great technical center. At the same time, because of the Depression and related economic conditions, a job in the auto industry in any facet that was still producing was a true gem to cherish. The area including the adjacent Ontario, Canada, area was heavily populated with German heritage residents. Although the region was first discovered and settled by Cadillac and the French, the Germans began to settle there en masse in the 1770s. The famous Stroh's brewery, which dominated the waterfront location on the Detroit River, was founded in 1850 by Bernhard Stroh. The brewery was at the pinnacle of German shops and businesses in southeast Michigan. Many of the street names were Germanic, and the weather was not unlike the weather in their native Germany.

Born in 1915 in Detroit, Louis Hahnke was the son of a German immigrant, Edward Hahnke, born in Bremen, Germany. Edward's father worked for the Beck brewing company as some sort of engineer. Edward arrived in the United States in 1886 with his parents when he was six years old. In 1910 Edward began work with the fledging Ford Motor Company at the Piquette Avenue plant. His wife's name was Olivia, and he had a daughter, Margaret, and sons Louis and Henry. Life was good working for the Ford Motor Company. Edward took the required classes and walked through the famous Ford "tent" of citizenship. When you worked for Henry Ford, you either were already a citizen or were taking classes to become one, or you'd better find a job somewhere else pronto! When you graduated from classes and received your citizenship, you would walk into a tent onstage in your native clothes and emerge from the other end in a business suit clutching your citizenship certificate. It was hokey, but it instilled in people from many different nations that they had become US citizens. Past allegiances were left behind in that tent with their native costumes. Many times a fresh start is good, and that is probably the reason many emigrated to the United States—to start out fresh and leave the baggage behind. On occasion you can leave a gem behind in that baggage, something you should have brought along for its value later.

Edward would tell his children the stories of their German heritage. The family name was Von Hahnke when his parents brought him to the United States, but a customs official informed them "we don't have any titles in the United States," so the Von was dropped. They felt it was the right thing to do, and they wanted to assimilate into American society. They were part of a large group of the Von Hahnkes who left Germany in 1880 (soon after Edward was born) and stopped off in England for several years before venturing to the United States. He also told them the Von Hahnkes were prominent in the German military during the 1800s, at one time including very high-ranking officials. The Hahnkes continued to arrive in the United States during and after the First World War.

During Prohibition Edward would regularly drive a "throwaway" car across the frozen Detroit River to Windsor, Ontario, and stock up with a few cases of Canadian whiskey to resell on the Detroit side. At the dock in Windsor, when asked the export destination of the whiskey, he would always reply "the Bahamas" and would immediately drive on the frozen river back to Detroit. The car had to be one you could walk away from should the cops close in, so they would not have anything to trace back to you. Also, it had to have very little value in the event it became a victim of the spring thaw and went through the ice. Edward always said people would be amazed if they were to explore the bottom of the Detroit River in the channel between Detroit and Windsor. He claimed the number of cars on the bottom loaded with cases of whiskey would be mind-boggling.

During the Great Depression in the 1930s Louis graduated from Detroit's Southwestern High School. The family had fallen on hard times with the Depression, losing several rental homes they owned and eventually losing their primary residence. They called home the living quarters above a funeral home in southwest Detroit. Olivia did the hair of the female "clients" of the funeral home in exchange for reduced rent on the apartment. Work for Edward was spotty at best at Ford during that period. Louis going on to the university could not even be considered at this point. Louis worked some jobs as they became available, but he found nothing substantial. He was blessed with a stroke of good fortune when he started to date the daughter of Harry Bennett. Bennett was the notorious head of the Ford security division of the Ford Motor Company. During one of his meetings at the Bennett home Louis mentioned he was looking for employment, and Harry Bennett gave him a note in an envelope and told him to report to the Ford company store. Louis also got an envelope for his father, Edward, who was also instructed to report to the Ford store.

Apparently auto production was spotty during this time, but the company store was always in business, so they both scored steady jobs. Louis started delivering goods to the homes of company executives, and Edward worked in the store itself. Eventually as production began to steady, they would work at the Highland Park Ford facility. Edward was able to purchase a home on Strathmoor Street on the west side of Detroit, and things were beginning to look rosy for the Hahnke clan. Suddenly Pearl Harbor was attacked, and that changed everything. Louis was twenty-six, single, and in excellent health—almost certain to be drafted into the military. He was working temporarily at the new Willow Run Ford plant in Ypsilanti, Michigan. They were assembling B-24 bombers; every sixty-three minutes a new one would roll out the front door. The production of almost three million cars in 1941 slowed to 150 new cars produced annually by the end of the war.

Shortly after the draft was accelerated with the declaration of war, Louis was drafted into the US Army on October 21, 1942. His best friend since childhood, Edward Seewald, was also drafted during the same period, and they both looked forward to serving in the Pacific theater. After basic training, Louis was assigned to Camp Tyson, a newly built facility in northwestern Tennessee near Paris (home of the world's largest annual catfish fry dinner). After training in the fine art of barrage balloon management, he was shipped to Seattle, Washington, to await shipping out to Alaska, where the Japanese had invaded. Lou liked the army life—the regimented style and the bonus of travel. Prior to his entering the military, the farthest he had traveled was to St. Louis for the World's Fair. Now he was able to sightsee and was getting paid for it!

While he was in Seattle, Louis was visited by two high-ranking army officers. They had a detailed conversation with him about the Von Hahnke tradition with the German military and people. They verified the information his father had passed on about the pre-World War I influence of the Von Hahnkes on the German military and government. They also approached him with an offer. They indicated the United States eventually was going to occupy most of Europe and most of Germany by the conclusion of the war. The US Army had a Military Government Division, which would follow the combat troops into newly liberated towns and villages and establish temporary law and order. They would determine which shops were off-limits to US troops, make sure essential services were up and running, and coordinate the transition from the Nazi government to a democratic system. Because the Von Hahnke name was associated with pre—WWI and pre pre-Nazi Germany, it was thought that having Louis as a representative would pave the way for acceptance of the change by the older German people. He would receive an immediate promotion to corporal (one of them commented that was as high ranking as Hitler got in World War I) and his own jeep (yes, one of the new ones made by Ford Motor Company). At this point it was a very simple choice: get shipped out to Alaska or Guadalcanal to fight the Japanese, or go to Africa and Europe. He chose the European plan!

Once again Louis seemed to have unbelievably good luck. In the meantime Ed Seewald was assigned to New Guinea, where they took advantage of his pre-dental school training and put him to work on patients' teeth in a forward hospital. "Pulling teeth and dodging bullets" is how he once described the experience to me. Ed Seewald made out okay; after the war he finished dental school on the GI Bill in Lincoln, Nebraska. He returned with his wife, Lois, and due to the postwar housing shortage they lived with Louie and Mary in their house on Burt Road in

Detroit. Louie would joke years later that Ed, Mary, and Lois would wave good-bye to him in their pajamas as he left for work. It wasn't long before Ed started a very successful dental practice in Ecorse, Michigan, that went on for many years.

So "Louie," as he was called by friends and relatives, was off and running for the East Coast. He was shipped off to England. As promised he was issued his new Ford Jeep, and with permission he lettered it "Miss Detroit." His commanding officer agreed it was a good idea to use the Detroit name because of the connection to the Detroit area—many German citizens had relatives who had emigrated years before. In Algeria they used French interpreters, and some of the soldiers with Louie spoke French. Louie's knowledge of English and German were not very useful at this point, except to assist in interrogating POWs. From Algeria he travelled to Sicily after the invasion of that island and continued to train in the establishment of order after liberation. Later in 1943, after the invasion of the Italian mainland, Louie was sent there briefly.

Soon thereafter Louie was given two weeks' leave, and he was told that after he returned he would be in England for training. He knew this meant the next invasion would most likely be France and his job would become more hands on. While on leave back in Detroit he received a dinner invitation to Ed Seewald's parents' house. Matt and Cecilia Seewald had a large house in Detroit's northwest side at the intersection of Ohio and Buena Vista. Matt Seewald, Ed's father, was in charge of shipping for Great

Lakes Steel and had seen business boom with war production. At dinner Louie met Mary Joan Seewald, their eldest daughter. He remembered seeing Mary as a young child when he would visit with Ed; now she was a striking young lady just graduated from high school. They hit it off immediately, and romance began to bloom. Mary would later remark that her whole family was thrilled with the relationship, as they had all known Louie for years and knew what a great guy he was. Although there was a twelve-year difference in their ages, no one seemed to be very concerned or troubled by that. Mary's Aunt Loretto (her mother's sister) made Louis lemon meringue pie every time they went to her house for dinner, because Louie had commented he could never find that dessert in the army. I didn't know until recently it is quite the task to make a lemon meringue pie from scratch. I can still to this day remember how great they tasted. That tradition continued for forty years after World War II.

After the leave it was on to England and more training. Everyone associated with the Military Government Unit had to agree on the goals of the program and how they were to be implemented. The unit continued to train in the fine art of diplomacy and at the same time keep up their normal military training, to prepare in the event there was a sudden reversal and they found themselves on the front line. Louie was left-handed, so some of the weapons were awkward for him to handle, as they had been designed for right-handed use. For him to load a fresh clip into an M1 Garand gave the words *slow motion* new meaning. He preferred the rifle over the carbine, saying he liked the range of the Garand, and he kept one in a scabbard mounted on his jeep. He carried a Walther PPK in small caliber as a backup and used that as a pocket gun. He had won the pistol in a poker game in Africa. He believed his approach to the civil authorities after the combat troops rolled through a town would be more successful if he didn't look armed to the teeth. He must have had some combat experience, because he was nominated for the Bronze Star during his tenure with the army.

After the Allied landing in France, Louie began following the advance, assisting with the change from a Vichy to a free French government. He visited the WWI cemeteries and memorials while crossing France. He was amazed by the volume of the cemeteries and how large they were for each of the major battles. Having never ventured far from Detroit, he must have found the scope of the military cemeteries to be overwhelming when he viewed them for the first time. He often commented in later years how astounded he was as he toured the Verdun area and saw the memorials to the soldiers of the First War. He witnessed several surrendering German soldiers shot down by French soldiers after towns were liberated. Louie had the type of personality that would not be inclined to shoot at people unless they were first shooting at him—and even that is doubtful.

But all things considered, France was easy duty for Louis, at least much easier than what was to follow in Germany. The French towns had not been carpet bombed by the Allies, so when the troops entered they were primarily intact. There were just the occasional buildings hit by artillery shells or the towns where the Nazis tried to fight a rear-guard action in a suicidal gesture. With the bilingual members of the unit and interpreters, Louie was able to communicate with the locals and assist in establishing normalcy. A big part of his job was to assist in determining which business establishments would be off-limits for the GIs on leave. Many times the troops would be given a couple days R&R back in the secure towns. Part of the Military Government Unit function was to make sure the GIs were not getting ripped off when they were on leave. Louie told me the story of the time he was having a beer with the captain of his unit at the bar in a French bistro. t. The beer was ten cents (US) per glass, which was a reasonable price at the time. Two black US soldiers from the Red Ball Express entered the bar area and sat down, and each ordered a beer. The bartender/owner poured each a glass of beer and announced it was one dollar US apiece. The soldiers looked at each other and around, and then each put a dollar bill on the bar without a word. They quickly drank their beer and headed out the door. Louie asked the bartender why he charged the two soldiers one dollar when everyone else was charged ten cents. The bartender responded by pulling a trash barrel from under the bar and dropping the two glasses from the soldiers into it, breaking the glasses, and stating, "It's ninety cents for the glass." That pretty much said it all. Louie and the captain responded by announcing that the establishment was now off-limits and that all military personal in there were to settle their tabs and leave. The captain, who was fluent in French, told the bartender that all troops wearing the US uniform were to be treated with respect; otherwise, none would be allowed to frequent an establishment that did not comply. They put the "off-limits" sign on the front of the bistro as they left.

I asked Louie if he received a lot of resentment from the other troops, because it sounded like he had a really "caked" job. He responded that he did not get much resentment from the other troops, partially because of his age. He was close to thirty years old when he was in Europe, and most of the soldiers were fresh out of high school or in their early twenties. He said the age difference was enough to earn him the nickname "Uncle Louie," and most of the troops referred to him in that manner. He bore in mind that many of the troops were from small towns in the United States and had never "seen the bright lights of Paris" before or imagined what they looked like. Many received their first dental care after being plucked from a near-poverty Depression-era existence to one in the US armed forces. And while they were on a couple days' R&R, here would come "Uncle Louie," with a table reserved for them and their friends to enjoy at the local tavern. But unfortunately the good times always have to end.

After France the occupation of Germany began. The whole picture for Louie changed when they entered Germany. Now he was moved from "on deck" to the batter's box—it was time to make use of the training and the family name that brought him there. The first thing he noticed in Germany was the utter destruction of the towns and cities. It seemed like very few were untouched; most had been bombed by the Allies or torn apart during the rooting out of retreating Nazi troops. The remaining residents were primarily the elderly and young children. Many of the older folks recognized the Hahnke name and would readily converse with Louie. They told him stories of the effects of the Great Depression in Germany and how, due to inflation, it would take a wheelbarrow of money to buy a loaf of bread. They didn't look like they were doing much better now. There were many refugee camps set up to handle the homeless, penniless, and destitute survivors of the war. Gone were the days of the French bistros, with their beer, fresh bread, and cheese. Louie not only had to aid in the establishment of the military government, but he also was often called upon to act as translator to captured Nazi officers. Because of the swift move across Germany by the Allied troops, it was difficult to do a thorough investigation of many that were in civil service. Some that would be considered to be Nazi sympathizers may have slipped through the cracks because of the volume of investigations. There was an attitude that led them to sacrifice the quality of the investigations for the quantity needed to keep up with the flow. Through it all Louie could never get over the destruction he witnessed and the suffering of the people. It was not at all unusual for the streets to be occupied with begging civilians, trying to get food to survive another day. Prior to this German experience, his unit had been looked upon as liberators by people anxious to return to a life enjoyed prior to Nazi occupation. In Italy and France the return to normalcy was much easier for the most part, as they had structures in place to aid a return to a normal government and commercial market.

As Louie conversed with more of the local elders, he discovered more about his family background and why he had been chosen for this assignment. Elders told him they had served in the German army during the Boxer Rebellion of 1901 under Field Marshall von Hahnke. They related that Von Hahnke had been an emissary for Kaiser Wilhelm II and represented him at many state functions throughout the world. They said Von Hahnke, although highly decorated, was part of the pre-WWI group of generals that steered Kaiser Wilhelm II toward maintaining peace while at the same time keeping a strong military presence. They also mentioned a family "tragedy" that befell Von Hahnke, but no one seemed to have any details to relate. Louie did find out Wilhelm von Hahnke was born in 1833 and rose through the ranks as a Prussian officer on the coattails of Otto von Bismarck as Germany unified into a single state. Von Hahnke died prior to World War I, and many of the people Louie chatted with felt the generals after Von Hahnke used their role to promote active warfare and helped lead to World War I.

Louie liked hearing the stories, and it gave him some rapport with the sixty—and seventy-year-old pre-Hitler group. Germany was a total mess at this point. As General Patton described in a Los Angeles speech shortly after the end of hostilities, "Coming over here the first four hours, we passed over a destroyed land, utterly destroyed. You who have not seen it do not know what hell looks like from the top. That's what Germany looks like; that's what Austria looks like."

The war was over, and now Louie had to make some big decisions. The army offered him promotion to sergeant, an apartment, and a Mercedes with a driver if he would re-up for four more years. The Mercedes was a Cabriolet convertible model, one of seven made for the Nazi regime and for the top officials from Hitler on down. Germany was starting to rebuild, and the Marshall Plan would be coming into effect, giving it the shot in the arm it needed to become prosperous once again. It sounds like Louie once again had a real stroke of luck. Having a car and driver, an apartment, and what was essentially a PR job in postwar Germany—how could it get any better than that? He turned the offer down and opted for discharge.

After much consideration he decided to return to Detroit, ask Mary Joan Seewald to marry him, and return to his job at the Ford Motor Company. He felt at thirty years old it was time to settle down, and he was going to marry the eighteen-year-old girl and do just that. I think the destruction he witnessed every day was also a determining factor. For years he expressed his dislike of waking up every day to look out the window at destruction and poverty. He reported the streets were full of beggars living day by day. He never returned to Germany, nor did he ever express any interest in returning there. He returned to the United States and was discharged from (of all places) Camp Tyson in Paris, Tennessee. He had the feeling the army was none too happy with his decision to leave, as they let him out pretty much in the middle of nowhere. But not to worry. Father Edward and brother Henry (recently released from the US Navy) drove the family Ford down to Tennessee from Detroit to pick Louie up and bring him home. That's an eleven-hour trip now, and I can't imagine how long the trip was back in those days, prior to the construction of the interstate highway system. It must have been two to three days each way

Louie on one of his first stops went to the Seewald house to visit Mary Joan. Ed was back from the Pacific, as were her other brothers, Ralph and Chuck, who were both in the US Navy. So the all of them made it out of the war and were back together. Louie asked Joan to marry him, and she accepted, but she insisted Louie get the okay from her father, Mathias. Mathias Seewald, or "Matt," was always known as a man of very few words, and those were usually abrupt. He grew up in Pennsylvania as part of an immigrant German family, went to a university, and became a mathematics teacher. He was quite the mathematician. He related to me how he applied for his job at Great Lakes Steel. During a second interview an interviewer told him he was in a dead heat with another candidate, and he asked Matt if he could do something to demonstrate his abilities over the other candidate.

Matt suggested he could add a page of thirty-plus numbers, all in excess of 10,000, faster than the man's secretary could with an adding machine. They had the secretary come into the room with her adding machine, the style with the handle on the side you had to crank to complete each function. They both received identical sheets of numbers and were told to begin. The secretary was cranking away on the machine, and Matt was moving his pencil like a man on fire. Matt finished well before the secretary and presented his total to the interviewer. After the secretary presented her total to the interviewer, he turned to Matt and said, "I have some bad news for you. Your total is incorrect." Matt, unfazed, asked him to have the secretary re-add the numbers at a leisurely pace. She redid the numbers and arrived at the same total as Matt did—and he was hired!

Of course Matt was a bit different with family compared to his business persona. He had a deep voice and a habit of reading the daily newspaper while people spoke to him. When someone finished with a spiel, he would look over the newspaper or book he was reading, make a brief comment, and return to reading. Louie had to get all of the courage he had up to make this presentation! He finally approached Matt and made his presentation as Matt continued to read the afternoon newspaper. At the conclusion of his presentation there was a moment of silence and Matt lowered the newspaper and smiled, saying, "That's the best damn news I have heard in years!" and returned to reading.

Getting married also involved a commitment to the Catholic faith, something Louie had been very big on for years. His mother-in-law-to-be usually went to daily Mass; I don't know why her car had a radio, because anytime we went anywhere in it, we had to have the radio off and pray the rosary. So after Louie and Mary Joan were married, they were regulars at Sunday Mass and the Holy Days of Obligation. Louie embraced his Catholic faith and was active in his parish church. He told me it was partially because of what he saw in Germany and the realization of how blessed the United States is.

CHAPTER TWO

So Who Were the Von Hahnkes?

So now the question becomes, "Who were the Von Hahnkes, and what role, if any, did they play in German history ? I attempted during high school to research through local libraries the name Von Hahnke and anything related to it. The search seemed to reach a dead end. Was the story about the military background of the Von Hahnkes a family legend used to entertain the children, like a bedtime story while they were young? At that point it certainly seemed like it. In the meantime I was leaning toward a military career, but Louie strongly advised me not to join. When I became of age, the Vietnam War was gearing down, and once we pulled out of there, we would have a surplus of people in uniform. Instead I joined the Detroit Police Department. The wearing of the uniform and the military type of organization seemed to fit me well. All those years of my mother and father telling me, "Stand up straight; don't slouch," finally paid off. Louie never talked much about his wartime experiences in his later years; in fact, he surprised me when he sold his Walther PPK to Officer Mark Bando, a coworker of mine, in 1976. He had owned the gun for forty-plus years and never bought a box of ammunition for it.

I would have liked to keep that gun as a family keepsake, but he sold it on the spur of the moment (I would have out bid Mark!!). Louie passed away in October 1983 of lung cancer. I found out afterward through my brother Jim that Louie had been smoking three packs per day most of his adult life, and it caught up with him.

So we fast-forward. I moved to New Hampshire and ended up working for the New Hampshire State Police. Now, this was a truly spit-and-polish outfit! The uniform shirt had real brass buttons and, with the gun belt accoutrements, had to be polished every day. They expected the troopers to be looking 100 percent every day, as they were the premier law enforcement agency in the State of New Hampshire. I worked with some terrific guys, including Jim and Jill Player, Jim Massey, Jim Bennett,

Pierre LaGranade, Danny Gagnon, Dan Wheeler, Jeff Gagnon, Dave McCarthy, Ray Burke, and many others. Jim Bennett and I used to work the Manchester area, and we got together for breakfast every day. To this day we still talk on the phone once a week.

The "always standing straight" philosophy came into play here more than ever before. Trooper Roy Roberts of Belmont, New Hampshire, always used to greet me at meetings with, "Good morning, Field Marshal," and some of the other troopers would greet me in German (Joe Burke) when we met. I found the greetings amusing, but at the same time it spurred that curiosity about the Von Hahnke family history. The training with the NHSP was the best, and it was reflected in the professionalism of all of the troopers.

So we jump ahead to October 2, 2004. While on the Internet I decide to put the Von Hahnke name into a search engine to see if anything came up. Low and behold, a picture came up of three men in uniform going down the gangplank of a troop ship. The picture is labeled, "Kaiser Wilhelm, General von Hahnke, and Prince Friedrich leave the troopship *Rhine*.".

The troops were leaving Germany to report to China and be active in the Boxer Rebellion. I was amazed beyond belief. Could this picture be the proof that the family legend was true? I started to run inquiries using various search engines to find out anything I could about the Von Hahnke family that remained in Germany.

I tried the search engines focused on finding your ancestors, but they seemed to be primarily for US family history. I continued to use standard search engines, using the terms Hahnke or Von Hahnke, and I would end up with a variety of results. Not only do items appear on the Internet, but they also can disappear. Case in point: the troopship picture. I did print a copy of it when I first found it in 2004. I could not find it for a while, but recently I saw that is was back up again.

I began to print all information I found, as I learned it might be online only for a time. One consistent source of information is The New York Times online. While searching under Von Hahnke I was directed to a site titled, "Hahnke Affair." The site had a detailed description of the death of General Wilhelm von Hahnke's son, Lt. Gustav von Hahnke, in Odda, Norway, while the son was there on duty with the royal yacht. Up to this point my search seemed to be looking at a successful military career of General von Hahnke, but this information regarding his son brought a new focus to my search. So I began to search for more information regarding Gustav and Wilhelm von Hahnke in order to find a base for the family history.

The Prussian Machine has a short biography on Wilhelm Gustav Karl Bernard von Hahnke stating he was born in Berlin on October 1, 1833. He began his military career as second lieutenant in a Grenadier regiment in Berlin. During the Danish-Prussian War of 1864, he was a company commander.

During the Austro-Prussian War of 1866, he was a member of the crown prince's general staff. He also was a member of the general staff during the 1870-71 Franco-Prussian War and marched through Paris when the Germans occupied France during that war. He was chief of Kaiser Wilhelm's military cabinet from 1888 to 1901, and in January 1905 he was promoted to grand field marshal and appointed Kaiser Wilhelm's general adjutant. He passed away on February 8, 1912. The article also mentioned that Wilhelm was Alfred von Schlieffen's son-in-law. This little nugget of information was probably the most important part of the article, and it will come into play later in our investigation.

I found many articles mentioning Wilhelm von Hahnke, but most were short and were not detailed. I will try to put some of them together as I found them on Internet. Wilhelm apparently ingratiated himself with the young Kaiser Wilhelm II when the future kaiser was in the officer corps taking military training. Reportedly he was impressed by Von Hahnke's military bearing and sense of humor. Wilhelm von Hahnke apparently attached himself to the kaiser's coattails and never let go. Von Hahnke reportedly was friends with Friedrich I, Kaiser Wilhelm's father. Von Hahnke was the same age as Friedrich and was active as part of his military staff. Upon the death of Kaiser Wilhelm I, Prince Friedrich became Kaiser Friedrich. Kaiser Friedrich reigned for eighty-eight days before dying of cancer. Wilhelm II was the new kaiser at twenty-nine years old and took on Von Hahnke as his adviser. Von Hahnke was fifty-five years old at the time and had much contact with Wilhelm while he was Frederich's adviser. With another general in the same mature age bracket, Alfred von Schlieffen (Von Hahnke's father-in-law), Wilhelm had a couple of "uncles" to give him advice and direction for the military of Germany. They were people the kaiser could trust, and they could be his representatives at state functions. Wilhelm II appointed Wilhelm von Hahnke as his first chief of the military cabinet.

Wilhelm von Hahnke was a relative newcomer to the nobility game, his father having been ennobled in 1836. The kaiser viewed Von Hahnke as experienced and having attention to detail. Tall and striking in appearance the kaiser later described him as a crystalline character with remorseless strictness. He was in the view of the kaiser the "perfect soldier."

Wilhelm von Hahnke definitely was at the right place at the right time. It is a challenge to find a picture of Kaiser Wilhelm II not in a military uniform during any of his state appearances. The post of his head military adviser must have been a prestigious job, to say the least! His friend and former coworker at the military academy, Alfred von Schlieffen, followed him as chief of staff, serving from 1891 to 1905. Von Hahnke remained the most influential of the generals and had the ear of the kaiser in most matters.

An April 1893 article in *The New York Times* cites a trip to the Vatican by Kaiser Wilhelm II and his entourage. Von Hahnke is mentioned several times in the article as being a part of the royal party. He was well known for his excellent taste in food and wine, and the kaiser apparently valued his opinion in those pursuits very highly. Von Hahnke was extremely conservative in all of his opinions dealing with the military, and he expressed those views to the kaiser at every opportunity. During this period, the German army was undergoing a number of changes to keep up with modernizing armies all over the world. Infantry rifles were undergoing drastic changes during this period. The single-shot rifle was being replaced by the magazine-fed rifle, increasing the firepower of the soldier many times over. The model 1888 rifle was adopted and put Germany back in the front, with firepower to equal to that of any adversary. The machine gun initially was ignored because it was considered to be only a defensive weapon. The policy of Von Schlieffen was that the army was always to be on the offensive and should never consider being on the defense. Eventually the machine gun was accepted and found to be adaptable for both offense and defense.

They also needed to make adjustments in regard to their canons in the artillery brigades. The French recently had begun to mass-produce their smokeless powder 75 mm rapid-firing canon, and Germany needed to catch up. The German parliament was hesitant to fund some of these changes to modern equipment, which also made the task challenging. The time period of 1888 to 1908 saw dramatic changes in military armaments and modernization of the German army under the leadership of Von Hahnke. The Reich's revolver was replaced by the Mauser P96 and eventually by the Luger in 1908. The German military was abandoning the revolver for a magazine-fed pistol because of the ease of handling and the capacity of the magazine. The P96 was also eventually adapted to full automatic (1932) fire, giving it the potential of sweeping an area clean. The P08 Luger, which succeeded the C96, was truly a work of art when it comes to pistols. It had a toggle charging system for feeding fresh ammunition and ejecting used cases. It has the feel like that of no other handgun, having perfect balance. It is said if you look at a target with the Luger at your side in your hand, close your eyes, and bring the pistol up and fire at the target, you will hit the target nine out of ten times. The pistol has the date of manufacture on the top of the pistol at the base of the barrel. Most of the parts are numbered, and the numbers are readily visible. This makes it easy for the collector to verify that all of the parts are original. The Luger was made in a four-inch barrel for the army, a six-inch barrel for the navy version, and a seven-and-three-quarter-inch barrel for the "artillery" version. That gun ended up having so many different versions it is amazing! They made versions with a "snail drum" high-capacity magazine and a version with a lug on the back strap for a removable shoulder stock that doubled as a holster. I bought a Luger dated 1912, the same year Wilhelm von Hahnke passed away, and it is the pride of my collection.

The infantry rifle was standardized in 1898, and the K98 became standard issue. The Luger and the K98 were to become relied-upon standards for many years, not being replaced until the 1940s.

CHAPTER THREE

The Success of
Von Hahnke Continues

Von Hahnke also was intensely convinced that the autonomy of the army included insisting courts marshal be held in private and their results be withheld from the public to protect the image of the military. He accompanied the kaiser to London, United Kingdom, for the golden jubilee of the kaiser's grandmother, Queen Elizabeth. He seemed to be part of the traveling group of elites chosen by the kaiser to aid him in representing Germany. The kaiser also wanted to surround himself with tall powerful men to balance out his weaknesses. His left arm had been injured at birth and was nonfunctional. The kaiser had to have someone else cut his meat at meals, and he needed assistance even in dressing himself. Was the constant wearing of military uniforms to distract others from the appearance of his arm? If so, it apparently worked; all of the decorations and trim work on a uniform could certainly be distracting.

In 1890 Kaiser Wilhelm II sent Von Hahnke to talk Otto von Bismarck into resigning from his government post. Hahnke spoke with Bismarck, but he refused to budge. Hahnke kept the pressure on, and a couple days later Hahnke presented the kaiser with Bismarck's letter of resignation. Bavarian newspapers reported that the general had a Knights of the Holy Grail type of relationship with the kaiser, with unshakeable loyalty. Hahnke and Von Schlieffen were his most trusted and loyal followers/advisers. Both were twenty-five to thirty years older than Kaiser Wilhelm II, and it appears he looked upon them for fatherly advice.

A newspaper article dated June 27, 1900, in *The New York Times* stated, "General von Hahnke, hitherto chief of military cabinet of Emperor William, has been given a high-salaried appointment as president of the newly created Imperial Military Court. The position carries life tenure." At that time Wilhelm was sixty-seven years old, apparently locked in a high-salaried lifetime job (pension???) as a reward for years of service. The military court would handle courts marshal and related items. Wilhelm had been pressing for years to keep military tribunes and their proceedings concealed from the public and civil authorities. This appointment indicates he prevailed with the kaiser and was put in charge of that function.

Because of the utter destruction caused by World War II, very few records are available regarding German genealogy in the period 1700-1945. One of my old tactics to determine the family of a person was to reference old death notices and see whom they listed as family and go on from there. They usually list immediate family and their city and state of residence. Also, one could estimate ages of the subjects until a more exact method was found. Because the family resided in Berlin, there are no records to fall back on. A number of newspaper articles are available from the United Kingdom and the United States giving us a little snapshot into the popularity of Field Marshal von Hahnke, including the following:

The Hour, United Kingdom
May 22, 1873

Detailed the actions of then Major von Hahnke during a campaign in the Franco-German War before he entered Paris with the rest of the victorious army. The use of the German superior railway system gave them a definite advantage over the French.

Local Government Gazette
August 28, 1890

General von Hahnke recipient of Orthodox snuff box bearing portrait of Czar Nicholas during trip to St. Petersburg, Russia, while accompanying Kaiser Wilhelm II on trip.

Amid a blaze of illuminations and a profuse interchange of compliments the German emperor's visit to the czar came to an end on Saturday night. Orders have been distributed with a lavish hand, and the orthodox snuff box, bearing a portrait of the czar himself, set in brilliants, has not been wanting to the occasion. General von Hahnke, the chief of the emperor's military cabinet, was the recipient of this special favor.

Centralia Enterprise, Centralia, Wisconsin
July 4, 1891

"Plans for the Kaiser's Pleasure on London Visit>"
London, June 27

Plans for the royal reception and entertainment of the German emperor and empress are nearly completed. Attended by General von Hahnke, General Yon Wittich, Count Eulenberg,

Baron von Marshal, Countess Brockdor, they will arrive in the Thames on board the imperial yacht *Hohenzollern* on Saturday, July 4, and be met by members of the royal family. They will be escorted at once to Windsor, where several apartments have been readied for them in the castle. On the following Monday the queen and the entire royal family will attend the marriage of Prince Albert and Princess Louise. On Wednesday, July 8, their visitors will attend a garden party hosted by Prince Christian.

Decatur Daily Republican
April 23, 1893

General von Hahnke had luncheon with the kaiser and the pope at Vatican City in Rome.

Boston Daily Globe
June 22, 1894

Scandal in Berlin

Society Leaders Received Infamous Letters.
Emperor William Himself Played the Part of Detective.
Arrest of Royal Chamberlain Causes Enormous Sensation.

Berlin, June 23

For some time past some of the distinguished personages in Berlin have been receiving anonymous letters containing the most infamous s accusations and conveying dire threats. The emperor interested himself in detecting the author of these scandalous letters, and as a result of his investigation he personally caused the arrest of his own chamberlain, Von Kotze, whom he charges with the offense. General von Hahnke, chief of the emperor's military staff, made the arrest, driving to the chamberlain's residence in a state carriage for that purpose. The prisoner was put into the carriage and driven to the military prison in Lindenstrasse. The arrest has created an enormous sensation.

Could this be the first arrest with the Von Hahnke family as lawmen? Could this incident have portended the lawman future in store for me? One of the other Hahnke relatives, Bob Hahnke, of the generation before me, was the chief of police for Ecorse, Michigan, for years until his retirement. Perhaps this "arrest" was a precursor of the future?

Daily Sun, Lowell, Massachusetts
September 9, 1896

Berlin September 9

The czar has decorated General von Hahnke, chief of the German military cabinet with the Order of St. Andrew.

Once again Von Hahnke is recognized for his role as peacekeeper and acknowledged by the head of state of Russia and the cousin of the kaiser. Another example of the "Henry Kissinger" of the 1800s!

Daily Mail, London, United Kingdom
September 15, 1896

Berlin, September 15

After the parade on the Ternpelhof field Emperor William made a speech to the superior officers present in which he declared that he was desirous of showing his unimpaired confidence in his loyal and valued servant, General von Hahnke, in face of the insinuations and attacks made upon him in connection with the resignation of General Bronsart von Schellendorf as secretary of war. The emperor continued that he had therefore appointed General von Hahnke to the conoloncy of the Priuz Karl grenadiers.

It sounds like there was some trouble in paradise, but the kaiser spoke out for Von Hahnke and at a time of criticism showed his confidence by awarding a promotion. This is another example of the loyalty between the kaiser and his lead generals. If the kaiser had any plans to discard Von Hahnke, this would have been the perfect opportunity. He chose instead to endorse Von Hahnke with another promotion.

Daily Advocate, Newark NJ
October 26, 1896

The Hague, October 26

Queen Wilhemina took her first communion in the presence of her mother, the queen regent, the court, and a large concourse of people. General von Hahnke has arrived with a gift from Emperor William for the young queen.

Chosen as personal representative of Kaiser Wilhelm II, Von Hahnke represented him in the royal court of the Netherlands. The kaiser had enough confidence in Von Hahnke to send him as his representative to other royalty in Europe and beyond.

Transcript, North Adams, Massachusetts
January 25, 1897

Against Socialism

Emperor William to Return to a Policy of Repression.

Berlin, January 5

The emperor's allusion at a recent court dinner to the reported existence of a court cabal and his statement that he knew nothing of any such clique has been said to not alter the fact that besides his majesty's public ministerial council, he has his all-important private advisers. The influence of General von Hahnke appears now in the ascendance with the kaiser, who has on several recent occasions dined with his chief of the military cabinet alone, a distinguished mark of imperial favor and confidence. General von Hahnke's ascendency implies much. It means the active prosecution of the plans for increased armaments, and the sphere of internal politics (for Hahnke *is* no mere professional soldier). It also means a return to a policy of repression of liberal ideas and especially of socialism It is known that the kaiser has for some time most regretted the line he took in 1889 in endeavoring to reconcile the radical finds that they will not be placated on any terms but their own and that his efforts at reconciliation have been taken as a proof of weakness on his part. In going back to a policy of restriction of which the Umsturz will have the heartiest support from the Hahnke circle.

So now we have the "Hahnke circle.". It is beginning to sound like Von Hahnke was firmly entrenched in the kaiser's formation of policy. In looking over photos of the royal family from the same time period, I noticed a tall figure in the background of many of the photos. He was usually directly behind the royal family, following not far behind. Kaiser Wilhelm had been in power for nearly ten years, and it appears Von Hahnke was on his coattails during that time and was going to be into the foreseeable future. All things considered, if one were to latch on to a royal leader, it could mean a job for life. Not having to worry about the results of an election every couple years could make for some excellent job security.

At this junction of our trail I found that a tragedy upset the apple cart and made things change. Newspapers were reporting that young naval Lieutenant Gustav von Hahnke drowned on July 11, 1897, while on a summer trip with the kaiser on the royal yacht in Odda, Norway. Soon after, initial reports began to appear implying some mysterious circumstances surrounding the death of the lieutenant. I also found it odd that newspapers in the United States and the United Kingdom had extensive coverage of the tragedy, although it was basically the accidental drowning of a twenty-six-year-old lieutenant with the German navy during a cruise to Norway. Or was it? I will address the extensive newspaper coverage of this even in detail in a later chapter.

Daily Mail, London, United Kingdom
November 25, 1897

The sultan (Turkey) has conferred the Grand Cordon of Osmanlela Order set in brilliants upon General von Hahnke, chief of Emperor Wilhelm's military cabinet.

While accompanying the kaiser on a trip to Turkey, Von Hahnke received another award in recognition of his diplomacy efforts with the Ottoman Empire on behalf of Kaiser Wilhelm II. Unfortunately I have been unable to find the citation for this award and many of the others. It would have been nice to have a reason beyond the obvious for the presentation of the award. I ran into the same problem with the Order of Victoria received by General von Hahnke. We can document that he received the award, but the reasons he earned it remain a mystery. Perhaps the German newspapers at the time presented a more detailed account, but we will never know.

Logansport Pharos Tribune
1898

General von Hahnke represents the kaiser at the funeral of Baron Otto von Bismarck in Berlin.

Morning Journal, Fort Wayne, Indiana
August 28, 1898

The big army maneuvers commence September 3rd, under the personal direction of Emperor William. They include comprehensive experiments with pigeons, bicycles, and airships. Among the airships is one of an absolutely new type of blimp. For a certain part of the maneuvers the emperor will assume personally the chief command. His military suite will include General von Hahnke, General von Plessen, and General von Scholl.

It sounds like it was time to bring out the new toys and see what might work. The German armed forces at first leaned toward the inflatable air ship as opposed to the propeller-driven aircraft. Bicycles were also strongly considered as a mode of quick transportation for the troops. This is the year the new K98 rifle would have made its debut with the troops and had a chance to be evaluated. Germany already had as its most reliable weapon the vast railway system, which was able to swiftly transport troops to either front. One year later the motorcar would make its appearance at the annual military games for its entry as an implement of war.

Herald, Portsmouth, New Hampshire
October 13, 1898

General von Hahnke accompanies kaiser to Middle East.

Kane Daily Republican
October 13, 1898

General von Hahnke with kaiser in Mideast

The Daily Northwestern
October 13, 1898

Berlin, October 12

The emperor and empress of Germany started at nine o'clock this morning on their journey to the Holy Land. They will go directly to Constantinople and from thence to Palestine. The suite of the emperor included General Physician Leutpold; Count von Eulenberg, the grand marshal of the court; General von Hahnke, the chief of his majesty's private civil cabinet; Baron von Bulow, the minister of foreign affairs; Legation Councilor Klemet; and a number of other officials. The empress has with her three ladies of the court and Court Marshal Baron von Mirbach. The imperial party is also accompanied by a body of gendarmes and by eighteen equestrians. The gendarmes have been taught photography, and by the emperor's order will photograph everything of interest under the instruction of Sergeant-Major Guessow and Sonnenstuhl. There are 110 trunks in the baggage cars, many of them of immense size and containing the dresses of the empress. One enormous box which does not leave the emperor's vicinity is in charge of a high functionary—it contains valuable gifts and diamond decorations valued at four million marks for oriental officials. Only six horses were taken, and they are for the emperor's use. The sultan of Turkey bought thirty-six carriage horses in Berlin for the use of the empress of Germany and her suite. The sultan also bought in Berlin all the uniforms and weapons needed for the ceremonies, which has caused the merchants to rejoice.

It sounds like a grand trip! The article did not mention the length of the trip, but it must have been for a long time, as it sounds like they did not pack lightly. Traveling to the Mideast during October must have been pleasant, if for no other reason than the weather. It appears the sultan is getting to be a generous host as the kaiser goes to visit the Ottoman Empire.

Eau Claire Leader
January 8, 1899

General von Hahnke in Buckingham Palace to represent the kaiser in discussion of Russian Czar Nicholas disarmament proposal.

The kaiser sent Von Hahnke once again to the English royal palace to discuss peace and disarmament proposals. I have the impression this was but one of many such trips by Von Hahnke to the British Isles. Based upon the tone of the newspaper articles of the day, Von Hahnke must have done well dealing with the British, as he was a frequent guest in England.

The Marion Register, Iowa
January 13, 1899

Kaiser Franz Grenadier, upon the occasion yesterday of the jubilee of the appointment of Emperor Francis Joseph of Austria as honorary colonel of that regiment, gave a banquet last evening. Among those present were Emperor William; the minister of foreign affairs, Baron von Bulow; the chief of the emperor's military cabinet, General von Hahnke; the Austro-Hungarian ambassador, Count von Szoegyeny-Marlch; the Austrian general Prince Windlschzratz ; and Field Marshal Steininger. His majesty toasted Emperor Francis Joseph, and the field marshal responded and called for "hands" for Emperor William. A portrait of Emperor Francis Joseph, which his majesty presented to the regiment, was unveiled during the dinner.

Spirit Lake Beacon, IO
March 17, 1899

The most decorated man in Europe is probably Count August of Eulenberg, the marshal of the German court, who has sixty-three decorations. This record was not even equaled by the late Prince Bismarck, who had only fifty-four decorations. Count von Moltke, another much-decorated man, had forty-four. Among living men, General von Hahnke comes after Count August of Eulenberg, with a total of fifty-two decorations. He is followed by Prince Albert of Prussia, who has forty-four.

To quote Humphrey Bogart in the movie *Sahara*, "He looks like he won a lot of prizes." General von Hahnke picked up a lot of decorations in the three wars he fought: the Austria-Prussia War, Danish-Prussian War, and the Franco-German War. Apparently he scored many more during peacetime for his diplomatic efforts.

Salt Lake Tribune
September 24, 1899

The Dreyfus excitement has largely subsided here since the pardon, though many papers express the belief that the surroundings will be one day removed. Others say the end is wholly unsatisfactory. In military and diplomatic circles the idea seems to prevail that Dreyfus was indeed a spy, but for Russia. This has found utterance in many papers.

Stirred by the Revelations.

An interesting outcome of the case is the fact that the emperor, who has been deeply stirred by the revelations made at Rennes of the espionage system between France and Germany, the extent and elaborateness of which he has hitherto been ignorant, has instructed General von Hahnke, chief of his private military cabinet, to thoroughly investigate how and to what extent the system can be abolished or reduced to a minimum.

The correspondent of the Associated Press learns reliably that his majesty, above all, was startled by the fact that the military attaches of both countries, while personally men of the nicest sense of honor, had been so deeply involved in the scandal, and he instructed General von Hahnke to ascertain if it was possible for Germany to take the initiative in abolishing extraterritoriality for attaches and other members of the embassies, thus abolishing the most heinous and dangerous form of espionage. The correspondent of the Associated Press understands that General von Hahnke has reported that it is impossible for one state, especially a military, to do this alone. He gave many potent reasons for this view.

General von Hahnke was assigned another investigation. It sounds like anytime there was a problem, the kaiser put Von Hahnke on the case. The Dreyfus incident revolved around the French Officer Dreyfus possibly passing French weapons information to the Germans via an embassy. Somehow because Germany was supposed to be the beneficiary of the information, the investigation by Von Hahnke into this matter was likely very short. The investigation probably focused on why the matter came to light more so than why it happened.

London Daily Mail
December 28, 1899

The Alert Emperor. German Army and Motor Transport.

The nation has had a good many severe shocks during the last few weeks. It has discovered that its artillery is old-fashioned and that its soldiers have been held at bay by inferior numbers of untrained soldiers provided with modern weapons. It is interesting to read the German military newspapers, and to ascertain that the emperor, having provided his army with artillery—which, it should not be forgotten, is much more modern than even that used by the Boers, and which, according to those German military reports, would immediately put the Boer weapons out of action—has instituted inquiries which will probably result in the substitution of a more efficient rifle than that the Boers use. Not content, he is now busying himself in the question of mechanical transport for military purposes.

Backward England.

We in England, as a rule, regard the motor car as an expensive fad of the wealthy, and a means of swindling the clergy and others by bogus companies. In other countries—in the United States, Germany, and France—inventors and manufacturers are busily at work establishing a vast industry that has already yielded fortunes, and that is employing in these three countries two hundred thousand mechanics. The Germans and the Austrians, in particular, have gone even farther than the French in the matter of the introduction of the motor car for military purposes. In a Stuttgart paper, which is quoted by the *Motor Car Journal*, gather that Major Madlung has been deputed by the minister of war to go into this matter. To him the emperor gave instructions as to testing the latest type of transport wagons. The trials began at Quedlinburg and extended over the Hartz territory to Gernrode, Suderode, Thale, and Blankenburg. The baggage wagons, the largest of which was loaded with 4Scwt., had not only to travel over the good but steep mountain roads to Hars, gerode, Hexentanzplatz, and Friedrichsbrunn, but had also to go over stony and sandy field roads and loose ploughed land for long distances. The baggage and two passenger wagons, heavily loaded, undertook the daring feat of crossing the Brocken, from Quedlinburg over Hexentanzplatz, Trescurg, and Schierke, in which they successfully competed with the Brocken Railway. From that summit on the Broosen the four wagons performed the journey over Hosenburg and Halberstadt to Magdeburg in six hours. On the second day, at midday, they reached Berlin. A large number of onlookers accompanied the trial journey from the beginning to the end. The driving power was a benzene motor. The baggage wagon has the appearance of the goods van of a train. The passenger wagon is similar to the motor cabs in use in Berlin. The emperor ordered the wagons to drive in front of the new palace and made inquiries of Major Madlong as to their construction. It is said that the troop wagon intended for quick service can travel forty kilometers per hour. Mr. von Gossler, the minister of war, and General von Hahnke were present at the inspection. The emperor was not sparing in his praise of the unusual performance

So the gasoline-powered troop transports made their debut. It appears the kaiser and Von Hahnke agreed on the worth of these vehicles. They were tasked with a lengthy route and apparently performed flawlessly. Once again the German army came to the forefront in the field of military transportation. Previously they were up front with their rail system of transport.

The New York Times
June 26, 1900

General von Hahnke received a high-salaried lifetime appointment as president of the newly created Imperial Military Court. This position carries a lifetime tenure.

Von Hahnke had been trying for the establishment of this position for years. He was well known for his conservative views and his contention the military should handle its own judicial proceedings. He also wanted the results of the proceedings to remain confidential, which he now had the power to do.

The New York Times
May 2, 1901

General von Hahnke named governor of Berlin by kaiser.

Daily Republican News, Hamilton, Ohio
May 2, 1901

General von Hahnke appointed governor of Berlin by kaiser.
Was former chief of military cabinet.

This must have been a great appointment, most likely coming with the mayoral mansion and all of the benefits. The articles do not mention if it was a lifetime appointment, but nonetheless it was an important award.

The New York Times
January 28, 1902

Prince of Wales repaired to the armory, both wearing the ribbon of the Order of the Black Eagle. Crown Prince Friedrich William, Prince Eitel, and the headquarters staff accompanied them. His majesty was warmly cheered by large crowds along the route; and the cheers, led by General von Hahnke, chief of the emperor's military cabinet, were repeated within the armory. Later in the day his majesty drove in an open carriage, through Unter den Linden. The great crowds present heartily cheered.

CHAPTER FOUR

General von Hahnke: The Original Henry Kissinger?

General von Hahnke is now leading the crowds acting as a cheerleader for the Prince of Wales, the heir apparent of the British throne. It sounds like he was not shy at all!

Boston Sunday Globe
April 5, 1903

General von Hahnke Made Field Marshal Because He Took His Punishment Without Complaint.

Berlin, April 4

General von Hahnke appointed a field marshal in the German army to fill the vacancy caused by the death of the king of Saxony—was one as scapegoat for Emperor William. Some two years ago the emperor made a speech to the Czar Alexander II so fiery and warlike that there was an immediate outcry, not only in Germany, but in all of Europe. At that time Von Hahnke was the chief of the emperor's military cabinet, a prime favorite of his sovereign, and regarded as one of his most influential advisers, the closest man in the army to the emperor. In looking for someone upon whom to place the responsibility for his impolitic speech, the emperor fixed upon General von Hahnke and dismissed him. He was succeeded by General Hurlsen von Haseler. Von Hahnke quietly took the entire responsibility for the emperor's speech, and so impressed the emperor with his bearing under the circumstances that he was made governor of Berlin. That he is still high in favor with the emperor is shown by his appointment to the vacant field marshalship.

It sounds like he had to take a couple lumps to cover for the boss; we have all been there. Rising to the highest military rank in the army sounds worth it, especially since it was a lifetime appointment. This sequence of events could have been titled, "He took his beating like a man and was respected for it in the end."

North China Herald
September 4, 1903

General von Hahnke receives lifetime field marshal appointment from the kaiser.

I've noticed the *North China Herald* was always a couple months behind the rest of the press when it came to reporting an item. It's like they were receiving their news from the pony express instead of through a wire service!

Fort Wayne Weekly Sentinel
September 28, 1904

Funeral of Bismarck.

Friedrichsruhe, September 21

The funeral services over the remains of Prince Herbert Bismarck, who died a hero on September 16, took place today. It was a simple ceremony, although it occurred in the presence of a distinguished company. General von Hahnke, chief of the imperial military cabinet, represented the emperor; Captain von Schwindt, Prince Henry, and Baron von Richthofen were also present.
Von Hahnke represents the kaiser at the funeral of the son of Otto von Bismarck.

November 21, 1905

General von Hahnke speaks at the commissioning of German naval cruiser.

Cruiser *Yorck* commissioned into the German navy on 21 November 1905.[4]   At the commissioning <u>Field Marshal Wilhelm von Hahnke</u> spoke, saying, "Old wisdom, *si vis pacem, para bellum*—he who wants peace shall be prepared for war . . . may the guns and machines of the *Yorck* be operated only by men with iron hearts and an iron will, men who know no other order than to put their lives at risk when the might, the greatness, and honor of the German people are being fought for."[Ruger pg 237 Gronerpg32

Atlanta Constitution
February 26, 1906

General von Hahnke led marriage procession of Sophie of Oldenburg, bride for Prince Frederick marriage ceremony.

Berlin, February 26

Duchess Sophie Charlotte of Oldenburg arrived in Berlin with her father from Oldenburg today in a pouring rain. After lunching with the emperor and empress, the prince imperial family, at the small Belleview Palace, she drove with her grandmother, Princess Friedrich Karl of Prussia, to the imperial palace, cheered along the route by . . . thousands of people. At the Brandenburg Gate the duchess shook hands with the chief burgomaster and thanked him for the address of welcome which he delivered. The procession was as brilliant as court equipages and cuirassed and helmeted guardsmen could make it. The princess sat in a coach shaped like that depicted in the old-fashioned Cinderella pictures, drawn by eight horses, led by tall grooms . . . Marshal von Hahnke, the governor of Berlin, and Lieutenant General Count von Moltke, commander of the garrison, with detachments of household cavalry, preceded and followed the imperial family, and all the visiting members of the royal families. The principal personages of the government were assembled at the palace to receive the princess.

Logansport Reporter
October 15, 1906

Berlin, October 15

The one hundredth anniversary of the battles of Auerstadt and Jena was celebrated Sunday. Monuments were unveiled at both places. Field Marshals Count von Kaezeler and von Hahnke placed wreaths upon the memorials on behalf of Emperor Wilhelm II.

Von Hahnke represented the kaiser at another ceremony, remembering two battles in 1806 when the Prussian army was crushed by Napoleon, a couple battles I am sure the kaiser would just as soon have forgotten.

Daily Journal, Racine, Wisconsin
February 18, 1907

The imperial procession entered from the picture gallery, headed by a detachment of the palace guard. Then came two heralds, their scabbards adorned with the imperial eagle and wearing enormously wide plumed hats. They were followed in order by the chief of the general staff; Gen. von Moltke, with the imperial seal; Minister of War von Kinem with the unscathed sword of state; General Adjutant von Lindequist, with the golden orb, called in Germany the "imperial apple"; Meld Marshal Count von Haeseler with the scepter and Field Marshal von Hahnke with the imperial crown; and Generals von Kissel, Loenfeldt, and Hoepfner, carrying aloft the imperial standard. Then came the emperor in the uniform of the guard du corps with the insignia of a field marshal, his golden helmet surmounted by a silver eagle with wide spread wings, topped by a small golden crown. Across his cuirass the emperor wore the broad orange ribbon of the order of the Black.

Apparently Von Hahnke was still participating in the pomp and circumstance ceremonies of the kaiser at the royal palace.

Brownsville Daily Herald
April 10, 1907

There are only four field marshals in the German army: Prince Leopold of Bavaria, Baron von Loe, Wilhelm von Hahnke, and Count von Haeseler.

Oakland Tribune
June 9, 1907

Despite strong opposition of the majority of the German people against devoting more money and naval expenditures, the kaiser continues to agitate for the building of even more battleships than his own plans called for two years ago. Emperor William Jets no opportune from being adept in the But there are exceptions. to impress it upon the minds of those who come near him, that owing to Germany's isolated position in the world, she must have a powerful navy that she may hope to be left alone. Addressing the conference, the imperial messenger General von Hahnke said, "I am commanded to convey the kaiser's greeting to the delegates present. the navy leagu e which has now filled the kaiser with joy and pride. The kaiser hopes that the league will remain strong and united, showing the German nation an example of patriotism and spirit, which ought to prevail in public life."

To please their imperial master the conference then adopted "resolution calling for a quicker construction of new battleships than Germany had seen hitherto, and the appropriation of enough money necessary to give the country a navy equal to that of France within" the next decade.

Shows Love for England.

As a proof of the kaiser's love of England and everything English, he allowed his messenger to say that no sensible man thought that any power in Europe cared for the friendship of England for his own sake, but it was sought after only because Great Britain has a powerful navy which renders her a valuable friend and a formidable foe.

LLoyd's Weekly News, London, United Kingdom
June 16, 1907

German field marshal attends. Represents kaiser.

What should have been a brilliant military spectacle yesterday, when the king unveiled the statue in Whitehall to the memory of the late duke of Cambridge, was marred by rain. In his speech the king referred to his revered relative as "the soldiers' friend" whose "one motto" was to do his duty to his sovereign and his country. The occasion was rendered especially interesting by the presence of Field Marshal von Hahnke (representing the German emperor) and six officers of the Von Goeben Regiment, of which the late duke was colonel-in-chief.

The new war office was used as a place of assembly for all who were invited to witness the unveiling. Whitehall from Charing Cross to the banqueting hall was occupied by household troops, and the route from Buckingham Palace to the horse guards was also kept by guards. All wore their greatcoats, and the scarlet cloaks of the life guards supplied the only touch of vivid color to be seen, with the exception of the red ensigns with which the statue was draped.

All the members of the royal family drove up in closed carriages and, with the exception of the duke of Connaught, hurried into the shelter of the war office as soon as they arrived. The prince and princess of Wales, the princess royal, and the duke of Fife, the duchess of Connaught, and Princess Patricia, Prince and Princess Christian, Princess Louise and the duke of Argyll, Princess Henry of Battenberg, the duchess of Albany, and the duke and duchess of Teck. Prince and Princess Alexander of Teck, and the Landp-ave of Hesse were assembled, when, punctually at noon, the king and queen, with Princess Victoria, drove up.

King's Warm Tribute.

The queen entered the building, but the king at once walked to the platform which had been erected in the center of the road to the west of the statue. He was attended by a brilliant company, including all the princes and relatives of the royal house, the prime minister, Lord Roberts, Sir Evelyn Wood, Mr. Haldane, the secretary for war, and former secretaries for war in the persons of the Marquis of Lansdowne, Viscount Midleton, and Mr. Arnold Forster, and scores of military men of high rank. The German officers, headed by Field Marshal von Hahnke, stood out from the rest by reason of their helmets and light gray cloaks.

The duke of Connaught, addressing his majesty, asked him, in the name of the officers of the British army past and present who had subscribed to erect the statue, to unveil it. His majesty, in a clear voice that could be heard right across the road, said, "I am here to thank you, as chairman of the committee charged with the erection of this memorial to my revered relative, the duke of Cambridge, for asking me to unveil it. It is enough to say that the appreciation in which he was held, not only by his friends and brother officers, but by the army generally, inspired the project to erect to his memory a suitable memorial.

"This has been done by the officers past and present of the army, by his personal friends, and by members of the city companies. The statue which I am about tounveil will be committed to the care of the Westminster city council. I can only say that those who pass it will be led to remember that the late duke was the soldiers' friend during a period of nearly half a century, when he held high rank in the army and endeared himself to all ranks. He had but one motto— that was to do his duty to his sovereign and his country.

"To add one word more before I unveil the imperial, and that is how deeply I appreciate the honor which the German emperor has conferred upon me by sending the distinguished Field Marshal von Hahnke and a deputation from the Von Goeben regiment to show their appreciation of the late duke by taking part in today's ceremony."

The king then unveiled the statue, and hand salute was accorded to it, the band of the grenadiers playing the national anthem.

Wreath from the Kaiser.

The late duke is represented in field marshal's uniform, mounted on his favorite and holding his baton. Two German officers placed at the base of the pedestal two wreaths, one of white flowers from the emperor, and another of blue from the Von Goeben regiment. Mr. John Belchew, ARA, and Mr. Adrian Jones, who collaborated in designing the memorial, were presented to the king, and presented them to the German dignitaries. Then both were heartily congratulated. Following other presentations their majesty, they went to the new war office and made an informal inspection of the building. Field Marshal von Hahnke and the officers were entertained.

It sounds like Von Hahnke and his squad stole the show. Considering he was seventy-five years old at the time, he must have been in good condition to make the trip and the appearance. Wearing their Pickelhauben (spike helmets) and their gray uniforms, they stood out from the British officers.

North China Herald
June 21, 1907

General von Hahnke awarded the Grand Cross of the Victorian Order in Buckingham Palace.

Field Marshal von Hahnke has been decorated with the Grand
Cross of the Victorian Order.

This was quite an honor! According to Wikipedia only 121
non-British individuals have been awarded this honor, including Olav
V of Norway. I am disappointed the accompanying citation listing the
reasons for the award being presented is not available. I do suspect it was
for his peacekeeping efforts over the years. Apparently he would show up
at occasions such as this, as well as at marriages and first communions, to
maintain friendly relations between those nations and Germany.

North China Herald
August 2, 1907

General von Hahnke represented the kaiser at the dedication of
a statue at Whitehall in London, United Kingdom.

Trenton Evening News
December 29, 1908

General von Hahnke among one of the most decorated generals
in Europe

CHAPTER FIVE

End of the Relationship

Lowell Sun, Lowell, Massachusetts
February 8, 1912

Prominent soldier Field Marshal von Hahnke dead.

Field Marshal von Hahnke, one of the best-known soldiers in Germany, died today. Field Marshal von Hahnke was known practically to everyone in Berlin, where he was born in 1833, and served most of his time in the regiment of the guard or the general staff. He was a great friend of Emperor Frederick, with whom he went through the wars against Austria in 1865, and against France in 1870-71. He also saw service in the war against Denmark in 1864. He was chief aide de camp to the present emperor.

Newport Sun, Newport, Rhode Island
February 8, 1912

A Friend of the Emperor
Field Marshal von Hahnke dies in Berlin

Berlin", February S.

Field Marshal Wilhelm von Hahnke, one of the best-known and most popular soldiers in Germany, died today.

Field Marshal von Hahnke was known practically to everybody in Berlin, where he was born in 1833 and served most of his time either in the regiment guards or on the general staff. He was a great friend of Emperor Frederick, with whom he went through the war against Austria in 1866 and against

France In 1870-71. He also saw service in the war against Denmark in 1864. He was chief aide de camp of the present emperor.

Racine Journal News
February 8, 1912

Berlin, Germany, Feb. S

Field Marshal Wilhelm—von Hahnke, one of the best-known and most popular soldiers in Germany, died today.

It does sound like he would have won a popularity contest! I do find it strange the newspapers covered his death, but that was where it all ended. There was no obituary notice to be found and no coverage of what should have been a large funeral. Even if there was a large write-up of the funeral in Berlin and German newspapers, I would assume it would have trickled down to the UK and US newspapers in areas with large German populations, like many of the other newsworthy events did. One of the articles in the newspaper mentioned a "magnificent" funeral being planned. The only thing I can surmise is Wilhelm von Hahnke and his widow, Elizabeth, wanted a quiet private funeral and that was what transpired.

Now we get to the big part of my research on this subject, the marriages and births of the Von Hahnke clan. Bearing in mind their family history for a large part was in Berlin, the records of births/deaths/marriages are sketchy at best. Louie told me when he was in Berlin at the end of World War II, there were many streets where the tallest building was under three feet tall. Most people were living in basements under the bombed-out rubble of their former homes. There is no doubt Berlin was flattened as no other city had been before. Totally destroyed. Many of the important (at least to us) genealogical records were destroyed, and there were no a backup copies. Today in the United States if I wanted to find the birth records of an individual born in 1830 in New York and their marriages and death, the task would be as simple as going to the local library or the county clerk's office, which would have those records on file. That is a luxury we do not have in tracing German history. I imagine the same would also be true of Russian, Polish, or Japanese records. The Internet offers many different dates and players, but it is also very loose with the facts in some cases.

The trouble with Internet facts is that many times there is no substantiation for what is presented as "fact." Case in point, while I was researching the Von Hahnkes, the name Count von Schlieffen came onto my radar as being related to the Von Hahnkes by marriage of a daughter. When I checked several Internet sources, they said Von Schlieffen had no children. I did find a site that listed two daughters, Elizabeth and Marie.

Elizabeth married Wilhelm von Hahnke, and Marie became a nun and lived her life out in a convent. This information seemed more logical. Also, several newspaper articles state that Von Schlieffen's daughter Elizabeth sent her husband, Wilhelm von Hahnke, to confer with Alfred von Schlieffen on his deathbed. Now we have the other problem of not having verifiable records; few if any dates are listed. I read Von Schlieffen was married at a young age and his wife passed away after the birth of their two daughters, but no corresponding dates are listed as date of birth and date of death for the daughters. It is also widely written that Von Schlieffen remarried and had no children with his second wife. Might it be some of the fact presenters jumped the gun and referred only to his second wife? Where this makes the presentation of facts confusing is there is no truly reliable source to verify some of these "facts." Another "fact" I read on the Internet stated Alfred von Schlieffen was Jewish and was actively practicing the Jewish religion at the time of his death in 1913.

As I look at the picture of the gravestone of Alfred von Schlieffen in the Invalidenfriedhof Cemetery in Berlin, I notice a cross is prominently part of the stone. So much for the Jewish theory. As I go through the available history, I will present to you for consideration my version of what I understand and believe to be historically correct. I will sift through many of the "facts" available and try to present a logical version of the history leading to the event at Odda, Norway.

Our next subject of controversy is the married life of Wilhelm von Hahnke. As I mentioned earlier, the military cabinet appeared to enjoy a "Knights of the Round Table" type of camaraderie of men ever loyal to the kaiser. Kaiser Wilhelm was twenty-six years younger than Von Hahnke and Von Schlieffen, so I am sure there was a proxy father-son relationship in play there. Both generals were friends of his father, Kaiser Friedrich, and most likely were acquainted with Kaiser Wilhelm II since birth. When Kaiser Wilhelm II suddenly ascended to the throne, he kept Von Hahnke and Von Schleffin on, most likely to keep a sense of continuity. Does this action explain in part why the German military during that period was slow to modernize and did so almost as a forced reaction to the modernization of other world powers? A common practice among the titled in that period was to use marriage as a tool to keep the blood line pristine and to ensure the success of future generations. A good example is Kaiser Wilhelm II himself, grandson of Queen Elizabeth of England and cousin to the British king and Russian czar.

Let's examine the marriage of Wilhelm von Hahnke. He was born in 1833; that has been established as factual. After that things get foggy in respect to his personal life. Elizabeth von Schlieffen was most likely his wife. I came to this conclusion based upon several observations of "facts" presented on the Internet and in various novels touching on the German military during that period. It is reported Albert von Schlieffen married at a young age and had two daughters, and that his wife passed away shortly thereafter. He married his second wife in 1868. Considering Albert von Schlieffen was born in 1933 (same as Von Hahnke), he could have married in 1851 at eighteen years of age and had his first daughter that year (Elizabeth). It was common during that period for girls sixteen to seventeen years old to be married—look at Kaiser Wilhelm II's mother's age when married. Based on that thought, Elizabeth would have been sixteen years old in 1867. Von Hahnke was thirty-four years old in 1867. In 1867 Von Hahnke had his first child, Wilhelm (1867-1931). Following closely after were Gustav (1871-1897), Oskar (1872-1926), and Adolph (1873-1936). The birth of the children in rapid succession would seem to indicate a marriage for Von Hahnke early in 1867. This was significant, as it permanently allied the two powerful field marshals of the high command of the German military.

There are reports that Wilhelm von Hahnke II was married to Elizabeth von Schlieffen, but I have sincere doubts. I would estimate Elizabeth von Schliffen would have been substantially older than Wilhelm von Hahnke II, and I feel a marriage would have been very unlikely. A widely reported story of Alfred von Schlieffen's death reports he gave the Von Schlieffen plan to Wilhelm von Hahnke on his deathbed. Apparently Elizabeth was too busy to see her father on his deathbed and sent her eldest son. Many sources report Major von Hahnke was her husband, but I believe it is more plausible she sent her son, Von Schlieffen's eldest grandson, to retrieve the plan. Although I feel my theory is correct, it is not without its doubts beyond its merit. I do feel certain Wilhelm von Hahnke had four sons, and we will continue on from there.

This theory is redacted by me later in this work when I report coming across the obituary of Gustav von Hahnke and finding a different set of facts. It falls back to my original theory to go with the obituary (unless Larry David puts it together).

CHAPTER SIX

The Shocking News

So far we have met the Hahnkes, and although Louie had some adventures in Europe due to the family name, and the relatives did make it big in the 1800s in Germany, there was really nothing exciting about what I discovered. The family tree shows Wilhelm von Hahnke was brother to my great-grandfather Gustav von Hahnke. So that looked to be the end of my story; I had satisfied my curiosity about the stories my father had related to me, and I had verified that most, if not all, were true. But I must admit that, like that kid at a Russell Stover candy store with a fifty-dollar bill, I was still looking, hungry for that last little bit of information so I could close the books on the whole matter. I had printed and saved most of the information I collected and thought it might be nice to pass it on to my children someday. I kept looking for another piece of information, browsing the Internet in the hope of finding another piece of the puzzle. At the same time I was driven by a feeling there was something else I needed to know. It is part of my character after being an investigator for so many years that I know there can be a piece of information that will complete a puzzle and make everything clear.

Early in 2011 I ran the names Hahnke and Von Hahnke in a search engine. I came up with a hit: "The Hahnke Affair." Thinking it might be a testimonial from a former girlfriend, I opened the link. It was to a *New York Times* article dated July 14, 1897, titled, "Lieutenant Hahnke Drowned."

It went on to explain news had been released from Berlin on the death of General von Hahnke's son Lieutenant von Hahnke resulting from a bicycle trip in Odda, Norway. While descending a hill he lost control of his bicycle and was drowned in the sea. A massive search was launched with no results so far.

This finding opened a whole new door to my search. I first questioned why *The New York Times* would report on the accident of a junior officer in the German navy. I began to dig a little further into the accident and found the next day—July 15, 1897—*The New York Times* published another article, titled, "Emperor William's Injury."

This article stated the public was greatly agitated by the news of an injury to Kaiser Wilhelm's eye. A long official report was issued going into detail about the accident. A heavy piece of canvas fell from the top of the ship main mast and struck the kaiser sideways in the head. At the same moment a piece of rope struck him near the eye. It apparently left him with a left black eye and very shaken up. Based on the article, it made sense to me the event could have happened as reported. Bearing in mind the kaiser had a inoperative left arm, he would not have been able to raise that arm in a defensive response as most of us would when seeing a threat coming at us in our peripheral vision. If he did see it coming, the only response he may have had time to execute would be to turn his face away from the threat.

The *Boston Daily Globe* of September 3, 1897, had an article titled,

Never Quarrel with a Monarch
Otherwise Custom and Tradition Will Force You to Suicide—Von Hahnke's Death a Case in Point

London, September 3

According to private advice received here, most persistent stories, already hinted at in a very guarded fashion in Mr. Labouchere's *Truth*, are now current in the court of Berlin, Vienna, and likewise in London, to the effect that the black eye which the kaiser received during his yachting trip along the coast of Norway was not due, as alleged, to the fall of a rope, but to a blow delivered in anger and passion by young Lieutenant von Hahnke, and that the latter's mysterious death twenty-four hours later was attributable not, as asserted, to a bicycle accident, but to suicide.

If the lieutenant, who was a most promising officer, really took his life, he merely acted in accordance with time-honored custom, this being the only course for an officer to adopt who has been unfortunate enough to become involved in any serious dispute with a member of the reigning family of his country.

Emperor Wilhelm had already to his credit at the time of his accession to the throne the death of a young officer whom he had insulted, and who, after responding with a blow to the indignity to which he had been subjected, blew out his brains.

It was the game with the late King Alfonso of Spain, and with the late crown prince of Austria, while if it had not been for the intervention of Emperor Franz Joseph, his nephew, the Archduke Otto, would likewise have a death of this nature on his conscience.

He had struck in the face, while intoxicated, a young nobleman on his staff who had barred the way one night when Otto attempted to conduct a crowd of drunken boon companions, male and female, to the bedroom of his wife, in order that they might see what an archduchess was like in bed. Before the young nobleman had time to blow out his brains on the following day, the emperor arrived upon the scene from Vienna.

Summoning all the officers and garrison in the town to his presence, he addressed the young officer who had been struck, thanked him for the chivalrous defense of a princess of the imperial family, and thereupon continued: "I deplore the blow which you have received from my nephew. Of course, you could not return it, and it is impossible that he could grant you satisfaction in the customary manner in single combat. But I, your emperor, can give you satisfaction, and not only you, but all these gentlemen present."

And with that he strode up to his nephew and struck him with considerable force (for the voice of the old monarch was trembling with passion) full upon the cheek, Otto making no attempt to ward off the blow, but standing there to attention like a very statue. The scene was an intensely dramatic one.

Then he shook hands with the young officer, and remarked: "I am glad to have known this in time, for I should deeply have grieved to lose so gallant an officer." Before leaving he ordered his nephew to close arrest for the space of three months.

Lieutenant von Hahnke was the son of the general of that name, who was chief of the military household of Emperor Wilhelm, as well as the moving spirit of that military ring by whom the kaiser has until now been surrounded. But since the death of the lieutenant, whose body has remained in Norway instead of being brought back to Germany, the general has not been seen at court and is reported to have severed his connection with the household of the emperor.

Another story regarding the drowning came from *The New York World*, September 8, 1897, edition.

Von Hahnke Struck the Emperor?

Labouchere hints the lieutenant committed suicide after resenting an insult.

London, September 7

Henry Labouchere renews in *Truth* the intimation that the death of Lieutenant von Hahnke, of the German navy, son of General von Hahnke, chief of Emperor Wilhelm's military cabinet, who was drowned while accompanying the emperor on the trip to the Northland on the imperial yacht *Hohenzollern*, was a sequel of the black eye received by the emperor at about the same time.

It was said at the time that the emperor's eye was blackened by the blow of a rope blown by the wind. The official story of the lieutenant's death was that he accidentally ran into the river Grondalseld on his bicycle while trying to avoid a collision with a shying pony. Another story was that Lieutenant von Hahnke committed suicide because he was coarsely abused by the emperor. Still another story was that the lieutenant, stung by the emperor's sharp words, struck the emperor, blackening his eye, and then committed suicide.

Truth says today: "It is worthy of remark that the authorized version was most obligingly impressed by the officers and men of the *Hohenzollern* upon every tourist they met.

"The official version of the affair, in brief, seems to be that Lieutenant von Hahnke, who was accompanied by a brother officer, accidentally ran into the river Grondalseld on his bicycle while trying to avoid a collision with a shying pony.

"The river is a raging torrent from which escape is impossible, and when the lieutenant's companion came upon the area, all trace of Von Hahnke had disappeared except his cap.

"We have received a letter saying that on the day following Von Hahnke's death a dummy figure, of the same size and weight, was tossed into the torrent to test its effect. When the dummy was drawn in, it was found to be torn to pieces, and everybody agrees that Von Hahnke's body must have met a similar fate. Yet, since the appearance of *Truth's* remarks, it is announced from Berlin that the body has been recovered after being six weeks in the raging torrent, and that it will be brought home for burial in Berlin."

So the plot thickens! It seems a lot of accusations were beginning to fly, and a lot of conspiracy theories were beginning to emerge!

This story is from the September 9, 1897, edition of the *Cedar Rapids Evening Gazette*.

He Struck the Emperor.

Sensational Story Connected with German Officer's Death.
London, September 9

Henry Labouchere

Truth renews the mysterious hints which have been in circulation since the death of Lieutenant von Hahnke of the German navy, son of General von Hahnke, chief of Emperor Wilhelm's military cabinet, who met his death by drowning in July last while accompanying his majesty on his trip to the Northland aboard the imperial yacht *Hohenzollern*. In so doing Mr. Labouchere once more publishes the intimation that the lieutenant's death was a sequel to the black eye which Emperor Wilhelm received at about that time.

According to one story the black eye was caused by a blow from a rope which was being whirled about by the wind. Another story has it that the emperor so coarsely abused Lieutenant von Hahnke that the latter committed suicide. Finally, still another version of the affair is that the lieutenant, stung by the emperor's sharp words, resented them to the extent of blackening his majesty's eye and committed suicide.

And then we had this observation from London, United Kingdom.

The Hackney Express and Shoreditch Observer
September 11, 1897

I am still receiving letters in reference to the now-famous black eye which was inflicted on the German emperor on July 11th, and the strange death of Lieutenant von Hahnke, which happened on the following day. Many of my correspondents are gentlemen who were spending their holidays in Norway at the time, and they are at pain to repeat the authorized version of these historical occurrences, with which I am already well acquainted. It is by the by, worthy of remark that this version—with all sorts of corroborative detail, designed to give an air of verisimilitude to what might otherwise be a bald and unconvincing narrative—seems to have been most obligingly impressed by the officers and men of the imperial yacht *Hohenzollern* upon every tourist with whom they came in contact. One correspondent mentions that the day after the death of Von Hahnke, a dummy figure of the size and height of the young lieutenant was tossed into the torrent near the spot where he disappeared When the rope to which the dummy figure had been attached was drawn in shortly afterward, it was found that the figure had been torn to pieces. Everybody in the locality seems to have agreed that the lieutenant's body must have met a similar fate. But, strangely enough, since the appearance of my previous paragraphs on the subject, it has been announced from Berlin that the lieutenant's body has been recovered, after being in this raging torrent for six weeks, and that it is to be brought home for burial. Perhaps in time the full facts in regard to a very remarkable affair may be known.

And we have another interesting version from the London newspaper *The Black and White*, September 11, 1897.

The late Lieutenant von Hahnke, whose portrait we give this week, was one of the officers of the *Hohenzollern* during the emperor of Germany's last trip to Norway. He went ashore one morning with a companion to cycle to the Latefoss Waterfall, fell over a declivity into the Grondalselv —a rapid mountain torrent—and his body was recovered only a few days ago. Many accounts of the occurrence, each more unsatisfactory than the other, leave us in doubt as to what to believe. One rumor connects Lieutenant von Hahnke's death with the black eye the emperor received on board the *Hohenzollern* "the day before the unfortunate officer met his death," going on to say that, fearing disgrace for himself and his family—his father is General von Hahnke, chief of the military cabinet—the lieutenant took his own life.

Two other versions assert his death to be the result of an accident—the *Daily Chronicle*'s special affirming that the fatality took place while Von Hahnke strove to avoid a collision with a country cart; while the *Illustrirte Zeitung*'s special correspondent, Herr A. Bockel, has a delightful story: "Von Hahnke lifted his right hand from the handlebar to wipe the moisture from his face," the cycle swerved and crashed. Of these conflicting reports it is evident that all cannot be true. Which, then, is the true version? Shall we ever know? It is not likely, since, as far as we can ascertain, no official inquiry has been made into the circumstances of young Von Hahnke's death.

They offered a nice illustrated portrait of Gustav von Hahnke.

The *Middletown Daily Argus* offered this version in their September 15, 1897, edition.

Von Hahnke Buried.

Last of the Young German Whose Death Was Veiled in Mystery.

Berlin, September 15.

The funeral of Captain von Hahnke, son of the chief of Emperor Wilhelm's military cabinet, who met his death by drowning in July last while accompanying his majesty on his trip to the Northland, took place yesterday with full military honors and in the presence of large "numbers of military and naval officers. The ceremony, which was most impressive, was witnessed by an immense concourse of people. Beautiful wreaths were sent by the emperor and empress and by Prince Leopold of Prussia."

The official version of the death of young Von Hahnke seems to be that while out bicycling with a brother officer he accidentally ran into the river Grondalselv in trying to avoid a collision with a shying pony. According to the official account, the river is a raging torrent, from which escape is impossible, and when young Von Hannke's companion came upon the scene all trace of the unfortunate youth, except his cap, had disappeared.

There have been other stories of the cause of death. A week ago Mr. Labouchere, in *London Truth*, renewed the mysterious hints that there was a close connection between the death of Captain von Hahnke and the black eye which Emperor William received about the same time. The official explanation of the accident to the kaiser attributed it to a blow from a rope which was being whirled about by the wind one evening when young Von Hahnke was officer of the watch on board the imperial yacht *Hohenzollern*. According to one version, the emperor abused Von Hahnke so coarsely he committed suicide.

It seems like the seeds were planted to indicate a possible cover-up at the highest level of an incident which may have occurred on the German royal yacht. The newspaper articles kept appearing regarding the incident or accident.

Then there was this article in the Massillon, Ohio, *Item,* September 29, 1897.

Grim Story about William.

The German emperor is never so thoroughly happy as when he is concentrating attention on himself, and he apparently has not yet reached the limit of astounding pranks he is capable of playing in order to be well under the limelight on the European stage. This makes it all the more curious that one of his many dramatic entrances and exits, which was closely followed by the traffic death of a young companion, has been shut off from the public gaze by the curtain of silence raised only for a brief moment to show the august figure of the imperial protagonist in uncertain light dimmed by the mist of improbable fiction.

It will be remembered how a short time back the world was pained by the information that the imperial navigator on board the yacht *Hohenzollern* near the Norwegian coast had received a bad black eye. Elaborate explanations were at once forthcoming as to the clumsy flapping or falling of vaguely placed rope on one of the best-appointed vessels manned by perhaps the smartest crew afloat. Then comes the tragedy in the shape of the sudden death the next day of Lieutenant von Hahnke, a promising young naval officer on board the *Hohenzollern*, and the press of Europe was compelled to swallow the astounding canard that this young athlete, expert at all manly exercises, had landed and ridden a bicycle over the edge of a cliff into the sea.

All this goes very well, and the entourage of the kaiser may be recommended as artistic fiction of no mean order. But the grim story which is now muttered under the breath in the land whose loyalty is so sorely tried by the feverish fuming of Wilhelm the autocrat is of a much simpler kind. It tells of a young officer who, maddened by some biting speech or rough, impulsive wet-of the fiery kaiser, so far forgot himself as to strike his sovereign, and then, on the next day, seeing that all was over with him, took his own ruined life. If this tragedy be true, even in part, for has its own precedent in history, if not in grave pity. That needless mystery and careful concealment of the details of the young fellow's death, added to the foolish explanations vouchsafed to the not altogether imbecile world, that the German authorities should turn men's minds to the gravest interpretations, even where the issue is less serious, is most curious. The fatality which impels the kaiser to do the wrong thing with unerring accuracy, as instanced by the congratulatory telegram to King Humbert and the count of Turin on his late duel with Henri d'Orleans, is omnipresent. In this case the revenge will be certain although deferred, for Wilhelm has thereby ruined his chances of being invited to Paris for the great exhibition of 1000 —a trip on which he is known to have set his heart.

—Harold Frederic, in *The New York Times*

And it started to get uglier as time went on; many assumptions were being made by the press.

Edwardsville Intelligencer, Edwardsville, Illinois
October 15, 1897

The Kaiser's Black Eye.

Many Versions of the Accident to the Imperial Optic.

No more dramatic story has ever been told about a living ruler than the one which accounts for the black eye

Lieutenant von Hahnke.

Emperor Wilhelm of Germany brought back with him after having been absent for a cruise on his royal yacht. It is said that Lieutenant von Hahnke, who is alleged to have struck the blow, committed suicide.

Numerous versions of the story are current. One has it that the kaiser spoke insultingly of the mother and sister of the young officer in the latter's presence and that the lieutenant floored the young warlord with a prompt and vigorous punch on the imperial eye, immediately escaping and blowing his brains out with a revolver. Another version is that the kaiser reprimanded the lieutenant for riding a bicycle around the deck of the royal yacht and followed this up with a torrent of abusive language, all in the presence of a knot of officers. Von Hahnke is said to have retaliated with a blow before his brother officers could hustle him away and induce the emperor, who was crying wildly for his assailant's blood, to go to his cabin. This story ends with the release of Von Hahnke from the yacht after he had promised to kill himself. It tells how he lay hidden for ten days in a peasant's cottage and finally jumped into a lake, from which his body was recovered.

Of course there have been official denials in plenty. The kaiser's black eye was caused, it was given out, by a swinging block or boom, and the lieutenant was said to have fallen from his bicycle while riding along the top of a cliff.

At any rate, the kaiser had a black eye, and Von Hahnke is dead. The lieutenant was a member of an old and influential family, his father being General von Hahnke, chief of the military cabinet.

And the press kept on going.

The Daily Tribune, Salt Lake City
December 12, 1897

Wilhelm II and Lieutenant Hahnke

The Story of the Officer Who Resented the Emperor's Insult.
For some time there have been rumors of a tragic occurrence
on board the German Emperor's yacht the *Hohenzollern*, and
various extraordinary stories have been circulated. A French
paper, the *Petite Presse*, is responsible for the following, which
will not appear at all extraordinary or improbable to those
who are acquainted with the peculiar character of the German
sovereign:

"The emperor of Germany, as most persons know,
is subject to attacks of nervous excitability, which recur
pretty frequently, and during these attacks he seems to lose
all control over himself. Some years ago, while he was only
Prince Wilhelm," he insulted, without any reason whatever, the
lieutenant of a regiment in a garrison at Potsdam. As the officer
remained perfectly silent, the prince redoubled his insults and
ended by striking his subordinate. The officer resigned his
commission and then sent his seconds to the prince, who,
however, refused to meet him. As an officer is dishonored if
he cannot obtain satisfaction for an insult, the poor young
lieutenant shot himself.

This affair became generally known; it was bad enough,
but lately another incident, more tragic still, has occurred on
board the *Hohenzollern*. Every effort has been made to keep
it secret, and it is first made public by the French press in the
columns of the *Petite Presse*. When the various mail papers
announced that the emperor Wilhelm, while walking on the
deck of his yacht, had been struck with the end of a cable,
which had cut open his eyebrow and caused a congestion of
the eye, many persons, asked themselves what truth there was
in the report and if it were not intended to conceal some new
algarade of the monarch's. These doubts were well founded;
this is what really happened.

The imperial yacht had just entered the waters of Lake Landven. It was early in the morning, and the weather was magnificent, and all of the officers were on deck. One of the lieutenants, Von Hahnke, was exercising himself on his bicycle, an amusement forbidden by the rules of the service, but which a few days before had been permitted to the officers by the emperor himself. Wilhelm II, coming up suddenly from his cabin in a very nervous, excited mood, found himself in front of the rider, who, to avoid coming into collision with him, jumped off and saluted respectfully. Had the emperor really been startled or afraid of being knocked down? Who can say? He gave a sudden start and cried, "Lieutenant, take away that bicycle, and then go and tell the captain to put you under arrest for a breach of discipline." All the officers were thunderstruck. "At Your Majesty's orders," replied Von Hahnke.

The emperor mounted to the bridge where the captain was, with Von Hahnke behind him. Suddenly Wilhelm II turned in a fury. "Do not presume to mount these steps reserved for the emperor," he proclaimed in a theatrical tone. Then after a pause with his arm extended in an attitude ala Mounet Sully, he added, "You are not worthy to place your foot in the tracks of mine." At these words Von Hahnke became crimson with rage. "Sire," he cried, "I am an officer, and quite as noble as Your Majesty! I allow no man to insult me!" William was raging. "I will have your epaulets torn off. I will break your sword. You unworthy servant," he cried. "Servant?" demanded the indignant officer, advancing toward the emperor, who sprang upon the bridge. He was followed by the lieutenant, who struck him a violent blow in the left eye, and following up the attack, threw himself upon the emperor, and would have strangled him if the officers had not rushed up and dragged him into his cabin. Blood was flowing freely over the emperor's face and clothes, but he had grown suddenly quite calm. "Let court martial be summoned immediately," was his order to the captain, who, however, replied very respectfully that by the rules of the service, before a court—martial could be called, some form of accusation must be formally drawn up, however summary it might be. "Let him be put in irons meanwhile," replied Wilhelm.

The court martial was commanded for the next day. What happened? The next morning the emperor was walking the deck with a black silk bandage over the injured eye; but Von Hahnke was no longer on board the *Hohenzollern*. During the night he had been helped to a boat and had gone off in the direction of the shore of Lake Landven. On the following day the Berlin papers announced the accident that had happened to the emperor, the fable of the cable hitting his eye. Three days after, they published the suicide of Lieutenant von Hahnke, who had incurred, they said, the displeasure of his imperial master. In truth, the poor fellow, after wandering for two days in the crest on the shore of the lake, had thrown himself into a torrent, which had dashed his body to pieces against the rocks. The officers of the *Hohenzollern* received strict orders never to reveal what had happened; but such a secret is hard to keep. When they landed, they of course told some of their friends in confidence, and from one of these the *Presse de Montreal* received the above account, which will not be reported by the German newspapers under penalty of fourteen years' imprisonment.

Manawatu Herald, New Zealand
December 21, 1897

A Royal Murder

An Emperor Struck.

In July last the German emperor was voyaging in his yacht the *Hohenzollern* through the Norwegian fjords. One of the naval officers on board was Lieutenant von Hahnke, whose father is General von Hahnke, chief of the emperor's military cabinet.

Several members of the Von Hahnke family hold high positions in the army and government service. On July 10 while the *Hohenzollern* was anchored in the neighborhood of the Sandven Lake, the emperor came on deck while young Hahnke was riding around on his bicycle, a practice which, though forbidden by the commander of the yacht, had been permitted to the young officers by His Majesty himself.

The emperor on that morning had evidently forgotten this, and when he saw Von Hahnke, he called out, "Get off that wheel, Lieutenant, and report to the captain your breach of discipline. You will remain in your cabin for the next three days." This rebuke was given in the presence of several officers and in front of a line of soldiers. Von Hahnke did as he was bidden, dismounting with the customary words, "At Your Majesty's orders." But as he ascended to the bridge to report himself to the captain, the emperor called out imperiously, "Dare not mount these steps. They are reserved for the kaiser. You are not worthy to crawl where the chief warlord (meaning himself the emperor) walks."

Hahnke turned as if stung. He was white with rage. "I am an officer like Your Majesty and allow no one to insult me. I will report in Your Majesty's cabin presently and demand satisfaction." With that he started to go below, the emperor following. "You little upstart," cried Wilhelm, "I will have your epaulets torn from your shoulders and your sword broken as an ungrateful and mischievous servant." "Servant," cried Hahnke, and with that his right arm shot out and his fist landed on the emperor's eye. Then he threw himself upon Wilhelm's staggering form and was about to hurl him to the deck when the witnesses of the affair grabbed him and bore him aft.

The kaiser was helped to his feet and carried to his cabin. He was indeed a sorry spectacle. His eyes were bleeding, and he frothed at the mouth, while calling for Von Hahnke's blood. He ordered a court martial to be held immediately. Von Hahnke's fellow officers, to prevent a public scandal, allowed him to get onshore, after giving up his sword to the captain and donning civilian dress. He there wrote his relatives and friends, in which he told them he had engaged himself on his word of honor to commit suicide. He drowned himself, weighting his pockets with lead, and hanging a piece of lead on his neck. Upon the captain's advice Hahnke's bicycle was brought ashore during the night and thrown over the rocks at the falls. The story given out was, "The emperor was struck by the end of a cable snapping in two, and Von Hahnke lost his balance whilst bicycling on the edge of a torrent and drowned."

New York World
August 7, 1898
Covering the dedication of the memorial in Odda, Norway

Upon the rocky shore at Odda, Norway, where a year ago he met his tragic death, a beautiful tablet has been unveiled to the memory of Lieutenant Count von Hahnke, of the German navy. It is something more than that. It is a memorial for future wonderment of the strange code of ethics which irrevocably decreed that this young [officer] should take his own life, It is a memorial of the remorse and repentance of the emperor who drove him to self-destruction.

For the German emperor was present in person at the unveiling ceremony, and in the deep waters of the fjord an entire fleet from the great haven at Kiel swung to their anchors as the lost salute was fired. And by the personal and sympathetic order of King Oscar, the Norwegian ironclad *Harold Haarfager* represented the Scandinavian navy.

Last year upon the royal yacht young Count von Hahnke was commissioned as a lieutenant. He was a bright and lovable fellow, only twenty-two, the son of General von Hahnke, chief of the military council. The Emperor loved him; he has shown it.

What a surprise! It turned out the Von Hahnkes might not be so boring after all! I continued to dig and discovered a follow-up article from the *Manawatu Herald*, dated February 12, 1898, titled,

A Black Eye and a Death

What Is the Mystery?

What Is the Connection Between the Eye and the Death?
There has been a good deal of mystery about a black eye recently received by the German emperor. His Majesty sustained an

injury to his eye on board his yacht the *Hohenzollern*. It was said to have been caused by the fall of a rope from a mast. Many paragraphs went the round of the press as to the accident, giving circumstantial details as to how it happened, and on the day after a further paragraph gave the details of a fatal accident which had befallen Lieutenant von Hahnke, one of the officers on board the yacht, which was lying off Odda, in Norway. The young lieu-tenant, so the telegraph told us, landed from the yacht to go cycling on the morning of the day following that upon which the German emperor had received his black eye, and "on an abrupt declivity leading down to the Sandson Lake lost control of his machine and went straight into the sea, where he was drowned.

In *Truth* Mr. Labouchere says, "My paragraph a fortnight ago respecting the black eye of the German emperor unfortunately received during his yachting cruise, and the death next day of Lieutenant von Hahnke, seems to have excited a good deal of interest, but so far I have had no satisfactory response to my request for information. One correspondent of mine has been in communication with the editor of a well-known German newspaper. This gentleman, whose name I am obviously unable to divulge, does not deny, nor does he admit, the truth of certain statements which were put before him, but in his letter he pointedly calls attention to the severity of the German press laws and adds that he cannot supply any information likely to cost him six months or more." What is the mystery underlying the emperor's black eye, and was the injury to the imperial optic in any way responsible for the death of young Lieutenant von Hahnke? If not why should the details of the affair, if published, be likely to cost an editor "six months or more"?

The New York Times
August 1, 1898

Questions to the Kaiser.

Why Is He So Interested in the Mysterious Death of Lieutenant Hahnke?

From *London Truth.*

The mystery surrounding the death of Lieutenant von Hahnke about which so much was heard nearly a year back has been recalled to mind by the recent performances of the German emperor at Odda, where he has been inaugurating with a vast amount of ceremony a monument erected by himself to the deceased officer. The proceedings at Odda only serve to deepen the mystery. It will be remembered the official version attributed the accident to Von Hahnke losing control of his bicycle at a dangerous spot and falling in consequence to the raging torrent below.

Certain persons, including one or more brother officers of the deceased, were believed to have witnessed the accident, but the names of these witnesses have never been disclosed, nor, so far as can be ascertained, was any inquiry into the affair held by the local authorities.

Ugly rumors became current connecting the disappearance of Von Hahnke with the subsequent appearance of the emperor with a bad black eye—in explanation of which another strange and unauthenticated story was officially put forward. Then, nearly two months after the event, it was announced the lieutenant's body had been recovered, although it had previously been demonstrated by practical experiments that no human body could hold together at this spot for more than a few hours. The body thus discovered, after having been in the water nearly eight weeks, was brought back to Germany with much ceremony, and received a quasi-public funeral, in which the emperor figured conspicuously. Inquiries made in Germany at the time showed that German editors had received other versions of the story of Von Hahnke's death, but that they were afraid to publish anything on the subject.

Now we have the further extraordinary fact. In addition to the unprecedented honors said to him last year, the emperor erected and himself inaugurated a monument to this young naval lieutenant, whose name was hardly known outside of his ship and his own family at the time of his death. We also see the German press supplied over again with narratives strongly suggestive of official inspiration, detailing all the circumstances of the tragedy.

All information, however, as to the evidence of which the narratives are founded is conspicuously withheld. In one account it is stated that a brother officer of the *Hohenzollern* was with Von Hahnke at the time of the accident, but strange, his name is not given. An old man and two children are also stated to have witnessed the accident. The question naturally arises, When and by whom was their evidence taken? Was there any official identification of the body when it was recovered? Did the Norwegian authorities hold no inquiry before sending it off to Germany? Were the old man, the two children, and brother officer interrogated by any official or tribunal? If so, why has the result not been made public? The function at Odda, and the newspaper accounts of it, all have the air of being inspired by some more important motive than that of commemorating the accidental death of an unknown individual of humble rank. If that motive be to dispose of the sinister stories that have been in circulation, it is strange that such cumbrous means are adopted, while the much simpler one of publishing the evidence is avoided.

These articles were but a few of the many that were in the worldwide press following the incident. The kaiser reportedly was furious over these unsubstantiated allegations.

I also read several books penned about Kaiser I I and they seem to carry on the story of a possible suicide and add the story that Lieutenant von Hahnke might have faked his death in order to sneak off to the United States. I checked ship passage records of that time period and backtracked social security information for someone with a similar name or birth date and came back empty on both.

I ran the name Gustav von Hahnke and Gustav Hahnke through several search engines for the United States and came back with nothing.

By the 1920s most living Von Hahnkes had emigrated to the United States, and there were very few left in Germany. It seems like after the kaiser abdicated, the opportunities for the von Hahnkes evaporated. I did notice one mention of Oskar von Hahnke, son of Wilhelm and younger brother of Gustav. In October 1918 just before the armistice and abdication of Kaiser II, Oscar was awarded the Pour LeMerite or Blue Max, the country's highest military award. I could find no report citing the circumstances for the award, but I noticed he was rank of lieutenant colonel in the quartermaster brigade and he was a medical doctor. Could that have been the last crumb from the kaiser on his way out, for the family's years of loyalty and service?

I continued my Internet quest, as I still felt there were some unanswered questions about the whole Gustav matter. I noticed in one of the articles pertaining to the accident, a memorial or monument was mentioned. I began to research the Odda, Norway, location and found pictures of the waterfalls described in the articles as the location Gustav was going to. On that page I found the memorial from the kaiser placed at the location of his accident.

Inschriften:

> **Gustav Hahnke**
> Imperial lieutenant at sea on board S.M.Y. *Hohenzollern* on July 11, 1897, at the age of twenty-six, of a fall in the Grönsdalselv. The death was at this point.
> Wilhelm II
> German Emperor
> And the officer corps, S.M.Y. *Hohenzollern*

Now I was getting more questions than answers. What really happened to Lieutenant von Hahnke? Could an accident be investigated 115 years later and an intelligent conclusion reached? Was it really an accident, or something else?

My research led me to a blog from Per A Hols, a local Odda, Norway, resident and a historian of note. The blog was in Norwegian, but a translation revealed there were possibly five witnesses to the accident of Lieutenant von Hahnke: two small girls selling wild strawberries and two seventeen-year-old teens working near the rapids. There was also another German naval officer on a bicycle who accompanied Von Hahnke to the waterfall site. This was exciting news! To find that someone had done extensive research into the event was very encouraging.

I studied the pictures of the monument and found the Von Hahnke family crest. Even with extensive searching I have not been able to find it anywhere else. Now I had the knowledge it is preserved on display permanently for all to see. The crest features a sword across the top, a cross for Christianity, three stars for the three wars Wilhelm von Hahnke fought in, and the German lion. I recognized the lion from the Stroh's beer cans of old; Stroh's was originally the Lion Brewery. The stars are supposed to signify major military victories. So another mystery was solved: we have a family crest!

At this point I came to the conclusion there was only one way to properly investigate this whole matter, and that was to view the "scene of the crime." I had purchased no fewer than seven extensive biographies of Kaiser Wilhelm II, and in reading them I found that most had little or no mention of Von Hahnke, although he appeared to play a very large role in the kaiser's cabinet. Wilhelm von Hahnke served the kaiser from the time the kaiser rose to the throne until Von Hahnke's death in 1912. He secured the lifetime appointments of field marshal and president of the military courts. He was also the governor of Berlin; Dick Flynn could have taken lessons from him! Von Hahnke managed to weather all of the political storms and still come out on top.

His lifetime friend and father-in-law of Wilhelm's son, Alfred von Schlieffen was also a very important player in the kaiser's reign. Von Schleiffen and Von Hahnke were both involved with the officers' corps when they met Kaiser Friedrich. Like Von Hahnke, Von Schlieffen ingratiated his way into a virtual lifetime appointment with the new kaiser. Between him and Von Hahnke, the kaiser did not have to go very far for advice. Von Schlieffen appears to be the more serious of the two. Von Hahnke was always known for his humor and easygoing manner. Von Schleiffin appears to be more dour, and none of his pictures have him smiling. You can bet everything you have his nickname was not "Smiley." They seemed to be a good pair to guide the kaiser, and they were certainly providing mature advice.

I had played it out as far as I could go by researching the Internet and related files. Now was the time to plan a trip to Odda, Norway, find the facts surrounding the death of Gustav von Hahnke, and put this matter to rest. As I thought about it more, I remembered I had been investigating accidents for the past twenty-plus years. Why not put that experience and knowledge to work in this matter? I could research pictures of the road back to that time period, and observe the flow of the water and its temperature. I could research the bicycles available in the 1890s to compare them to modern bicycles. I decided to go to Odda and do the research needed to come to a logical conclusion regarding the death of Gustav von Hahnke.

Planning the Trip

Unfortunately, although I am a direct descendant of one who appears to have been one of the more powerful and wealthy men of 1890s Germany, I am not a person of unlimited resources. It was fun to imagine how the trip would have been made today by Wilhelm.

I imagine if Wilhelm von Hahnke were alive now and planning the same trip, he would charter a private jet to fly from Nashville, Tennessee, to Heathrow Airport in London, United Kingdom. The jet would have luxurious seating, gourmet foods, and attractive flight attendants. After arriving in London, he would visit Buckingham Palace and convey his greetings to the royal family. He'd probably do some skeet shooting with Prince Charles after luncheon and attend a state dinner in the evening. After staying in London for a couple days taking in the sights, he would be off for Bergen, Norway, in that private jet.

After landing in Bergen, he would relax at the Bergen Clarion Airport Inn, reserving an entire floor for him and his entourage. He would no doubt host a gourmet dinner in the elegant hotel dining area with the local officials and have an evening of shaking hands and kissing babies. The next day a fleet of limousines would take him and his party on the four-hour drive to Odda. The party would stop often during the trip to enjoy the scenery and take pictures of the countryside. The four-hour drive would turn into an all-day affair, and they would stop for a leisurely luncheon at one of the small towns on the way.

For the stay in Odda, he would have reserved the entire Vasstun Inn for the week. One of his aides would have ensured the inn was stocked with prime rib, lobster, and salmon for the dining delight of the party. The daily routine would include a trip to the waterfalls and the glaciers surrounding Odda. Also, the itinerary would include daily trips into the town to explore the shops and view the harbor, which at one time hosted the royal yachts of the most powerful nations of Europe. A tour of the power plant complex and the museum would also be on the agenda.

After a week of seeing the sights they would make the return trip to Bergen and fly nonstop back to Nashville International Airport. Upon arriving in Nashville after the luxurious flight and a six-hour nap, Wilhelm would be ready to go for another day!

Now we must pop the balloon and look at the reality of Robert von Hahnke in 2012.

The first thing of course was to check into the visa/passport issues. I located my passport and confirmed it was valid for a couple more years. I then went to the Internet and researched the travel requirements for entry into Norway. No visa was required, so that saved a lot of headaches. I traveled to China about ten years ago, and they required a visa. It was not a problem to acquire a visa, but the doubt lurks in the back of your mind: what if they reject me? I had reserved a flight and a hotel, prepaid, and being rejected would be a disaster. I started to think and arrived at the conclusion the only time I did anything that could be construed as anti-Chinese was when I laughed at a Chinese guy at the karaoke bar when he sung, "I wuv how you wuv me." I received the visa and had a great time in Beijing for ten days.

I was glad the visa was a non-issue, so I went on to the next consideration. When to visit is always an important part of planning a trip. When I was married in New Hampshire, we would take a trip to the Caribbean during the end of March, leaving the snow-encrusted land for the warm white sandy beaches. When we returned we had a mental refreshment knowing the snow would eventually melt and we had had a break from the weather. So the next step was to investigate the weather and use that as a consideration for planning the trip. The high temperatures in the month of July in Odda were in the vicinity of sixty degrees (F). According to the weather stats I checked, it dropped from there. Considering Odda is surrounded by glacial mountains, sixty was probably doing well. Also, the date of the Gustav von Hahnke tragedy was July 11, 1897. If I went in July, I could be there for the 115th anniversary. The airfare would have been cut in half if I had waited to visit during September or beyond, which looked appealing, but would it cost me on the other end with bad weather? I decided to go for the sure bet and go in July. Having been in the mountainous region of New Hampshire for twenty-plus years, I know how the weather can affect travel. An early snowstorm occurs, and travel is severely curtailed. One of the last things needed on a trip is delays caused by weather. That tends to throw off your whole schedule and leads to anxiety not needed on a pleasant vacation.

So we had our schedule set—the second week in July 2012; now we needed to to find a reasonable round-trip flight. Once again the Internet was the main facilitator for booking flights. I wanted to get a reasonably priced flight but at the same time not travel on a cattle car. I am six feet two and 225 pounds, so I need some room if I am going to sit for many hours of the transatlantic flight.

There are many sites on the Internet that will book your flight, all claiming to be better than the others. I looked for booking on specific international carriers that would be reliable and probably provide suitable seating. I ended up booking through British Airways. They have an excellent reputation, and their pricing was very competitive. I booked through CheapOair, an Internet company. The tickets were listed as Internet Tickets, and I received my itinerary via e-mail. The itinerary left much to be desired with the stopover schedule.

From:	Depart:
Nashville, TN, USA	Sunday, Jul 08, 2012
To:	Return:
Bergen, NO	Saturday Jul 14, 2012
FROM:	ARRIVE:
Nashville (BNA)	Chicago OHare
05:25PM Jul 08, Sunday	07:15PM Jul 08, Sunday
FROM	ARRIVE:
Chicago OHare	London Heathrow
08:35PM Jul 08 Sunday	10:00 AM Jul 09 Monday
FROM	ARRIVE
London Heathrow	Bergen
02:25PM July09 Monday	05:25PM July 09 Monday

RETURN FLIGHTS

FROM	ARRIVE
Bergen	London Heathrow
06:20PM Jul 14 Saturday	07:30PM Jul 14 Saturday

FROM	ARRIVE
London Heathrow	New York JFK
10:45AM July 15 Sunday	01:30PM Jul 15 Sunday

FROM	ARRIVE
New York JFK	Nashville
05:00PM July 15 Sunday	06:30PM Jul 15 Sunday

The air travel part of the trip was settled. As usual, I accepted the bargain over the shorter layover time, and I would live to regret it. While shopping for the trip I failed to look at other flight options with possibly shorter layover times. Two portions that concerned me were the arrival time in Bergen and the layover on the return flight to London.

Arriving in Bergen at 5:25 p.m. would limit my traveling farther during that day. Bearing that in mind, I made reservations at the Bergen Airport Clarion for the evening of Monday, July 9, giving me a chance to rest after going that far and before completing my trip to Odda. Having stayed at the Clarion Hotels in the United States, I felt confident the Clarion in Norway would also be up to the high standards of the Choice Hotels group. I had researched the last leg of the trip and found I had two options: rent a car or ride the bus. The bus ride was listed as a four-hour trip, which translated into a three-hour drive in a rental car. There was a large amount of information regarding the bus and its schedule in that region, but very little car rental information. Would I need an international driver's license? What was covered by insurance? Do they drive on the right or left side of the road in Norway? And last, was it a straight drive on an interstate type of highway or was it all back roads? Because of these many concerns I was beginning to favor the bus, but I did not want to commit until my questions were answered when I arrived. So I decided at the planning stage that the decision on how to make the last leg of the journey would be an on-the-spot decision in Bergen, Norway.

The next task was to plan the accommodations for the four-night stay in Odda. I had been corresponding with a local frau, Gisela, who is a photographer and lives with her family in Odda. She did not have any direct recommendations but warned it could be expensive. I found two hotels listed on the Internet within Odda. I liked the Vasstun Hotel, as it is located on the edge of town nearest to the Von Hahnke monument. They offered a variety of rooms and a variety of rates, and rooms with shared bathrooms and rooms with private bathrooms. I ended up with a double room with a private shower and bathroom. I was early enough with my reservation I could choose that option, and for a few dollars more it seemed like one more headache would be avoided. While planning this trip I kept in mind the fewer headaches I could plan around in advance, the better I would be when the unexpected headaches popped up (and you just know they do). The pictures of the Vasstun showed it is at the base of a lake below the glaciers with a view of several waterfalls. And best of all, it is a straight shot on the road conveniently located exactly twenty kilometers north of the Von Hahnke monument. The pictures of their complimentary breakfast looked good, and they had an on-site restaurant and bar. It looked like the perfect place to use as a base for my research in the area.

Next I had to look ahead to the return flights. The layover in London from 7:30 p.m. Saturday to 10:45 a.m. Sunday was going to need some thought. Fourteen hours was definitely too long to be lounging in a chair at the airport, especially in preparation for a six—to seven-hour nonstop flight. I once again looked to our friends at Choice Hotels.com and found a Quality Inn located within a few minutes of the airport. I made reservations for Saturday night at the Heathrow Quality Inn and felt like it would make the trip that much more enjoyable with the break to rest. It has an in-house restaurant and bar, so that would help make the stop all that more enjoyable.

Another concern was Internet availability during the trip to ensure communications with friends back home. Hotel Vasstun advertises Internet connection available, as does the Bergen Airport Clarion and the Heathrow Quality Inn. I knew the airports all have wireless, so that would be covered. I began to think about my cell phone and the pros and cons of bringing it to Europe. I phoned my cell phone provider, and they indicated that for an additional charge I could purchase a chip for my phone that would make it functional in Europe. I thought about it for two seconds and responded I would pass, as I could probably use a break from the cell phone. I would just provide emergency contacts with the phone numbers at the hotels I was staying at in the event they needed to contact me. But on the Internet issue we still had one concern: the difference in electric power plugs. Although I could have Internet access, I would need to keep my laptop charged, or the contact would not last.

I went on the Internet searching for an education in the power plug situation. I found that not only do they have a different power voltage in Europe, but different countries have different styles of outlets in the walls. The one for the United Kingdom might not fit in Germany, which might be different for France, which might be different for Norway. After an extensive search on the Internet, I found a site explaining in layman's terms the outlet plugs you need for each individual country. You also need a transformer to change the voltage over so your laptop won't crash and burn when you plug it in. I chose the Norway-style plug, as during the trip I was going to be in the United Kingdom only one day, and I could arrive fully charged from Norway. The equipment arrived several days after I ordered it. It seemed heavy and bulky for the size of it, but necessary just the same. That was the beginning of the packing for the trip, the first item I chose to bring along. Next our consideration in planning and packing was the ever important item of clothing.

The month before the trip, almost every day in Nashville, Tennessee, was one hundred degrees (F) plus! It was shaping up to be one of the hottest summers on record. At first the thought entered my head I might be able to get away with a computer case and two carry-on bags for the trip. The possible downside of that plan was every time I heard of a suspected terrorist being detained, they always wrapped up the news report with "and he was traveling to/from Europe with no checked baggage." I had begun to look at that statement as a tag they put on people implying there must be some guilt. Pull him over here, and check him out thoroughly; he has no checked baggage! Since I was going to be traveling back through three points of entry in different countries did not have an overwhelming desire to meet "Mr. McFeeley" in any of them, the checked bag started to look better.

I opted to use a carry-on that would easily fit in the overhead and a large gym bag type with a frame and wheels. It too would probably fit in the overhead, but why push the issue?

Moving on to the packing stage, I wanted to determine the type of clothing to pack. Online pictures from the Odda area showed it was definitely casual and a little bit mountain climbing. It was time for the great dictators of clothing to reveal themselves: the weather forecast and reports. On the upside the month of July is the warmest month in Odda. It is definitely the middle of summer. I observed the average high temperature in July was sixty-one degrees (F). It dropped to the high to mid-forties at night. That was quite a change from the one hundred plus of Nashville! I began to find my stored winter items and packed my sweatshirts, insulated hiking boots, heavy socks, and sweatpants in case they were needed. I packed those items in the checked bag, and that bag was starting to fill fast. I packed my prescription bottles in the checked bag also, assuming it would save any hassle during the security check at the airports (big mistake). I made copies of my passport and itinerary and put them in the checked bag on top of everything else. The bags were filling up fast, and I stopped to caution myself: The more I pack, the more I have to lug around, and it's only four days in Norway, not two months in Africa. If I don't pack something, I can always buy it there if needed. I also packed the pocket (needed some huge pockets) English-Norwegian and Norwegian-English translator. I purchased it at the beginning of the trip planning. I practiced taking Norwegian phrases off the Internet and translating them using the machine. It worked great! It looked like I was covering every base and getting ready for the trip to complete my investigation.

The packing was an effort spanning a couple weeks. I left the bags in the spare bedroom, and every time I thought of a new necessary item, I would place it in the appropriate bag. Should I bring hiking boots and a couple pair of casual shoes? We definitely need to wear a pair of loafer-style shoes to clear security in a speedy fashion. I always have felt pressured while going through the security line. Get your shoes off, open the computer case, open the computer, place all metal objects in a plastic container, check yourself again to make sure you have no metal objects on your person. In the meantime the person behind you is giving you the "hurry up" look, making you feel like a contestant on some sort of game show that you are losing. The loafer-style shoes definitely put you ahead of the pack. The guy from up north wearing the lace-up thermal boots is going to be in last place. I was that guy once, and I remember the huffing going on behind me as I tried to get the boots unlaced halfway down so I could yank them off. I learned the boots go into the carry-on or check-in bag, and the loafers are for travel to and from.

At this point we were all packed and ready to go. I left some space in each bag for those last-minute items that always pop up, but for the most part I was ready. I would need some items to measure the road grade at the scene of the accident and to measure the water temperature near the location of the fall into the rapids, and a report book to record my findings. Those items could be purchased locally at the Norwegian version of Ace Hardware in downtown Odda. The entry of Von Hahnke would certainly be more low-key than the appearances of the Von Hahnkes of the past, but it would be a remarkable trip just the same.

Last but not least, transportation to and from the airport needed to be planned. This has always been a sore subject for me since 1986, when I was dispatched by my wife to pick up her mother at the Manchester, New Hampshire, airport, a two-hour drive each way from our house. After driving all day in the state police car, I jumped into our Reliant K station wagon, and with two-year-old son Robert Jr. in the car seat headed for Manchester. As I left, my wife reminded me how her mother would not look favorably upon my being late and that she enjoyed the relatives waiting at the gate when she arrived to a warm welcome. So I left earlier than necessary to ensure that no matter what the traffic or parking situation, I was going to be at that gate with Robert when Grandma made her entrance. At the airport I was thirty minutes early, and then the flight was delayed another thirty minutes. Finally the plane docked at the debarkation station, and in waltzed the passengers. After all of the passengers had gone by, there was no Grandma. I waited for a few minutes to see if she was going to make a grand entrance after the rest of the passengers, but nothing!

I approached the ticket agent and asked if all passengers were off the plane, and she indicated they were. I gave her my mother-in-law's name, and she stated she was not listed as a passenger. It was the days before cell phones were widespread, so I had to tow Robert around until I could find a pay phone and call home. I was certain I was at the right place, as I had written down the flight number and arrival time as my wife got them from her mother. To my delight, when I phoned my wife she relayed that her mother had phoned her about two hours ago and said she had to take a later flight. I went back to the terminal and checked the arrival board; I had only another one-and-one-half-hour wait until the plane arrived. So for one and a half hours I walked Robert around trying to keep him amused. Finally after what seemed like forever, the flight arrived and Loraine made her appearance. We were in the car headed back when she went into detail concerning the late flight. Apparently the plane in Raleigh, North Carolina, was overbooked, and they asked for volunteers to take a later flight for a one-hundred-dollar discount coupon on a future flight. She told me how she jumped up and had to beat a man to the counter so she could get the offer. I was astounded! I knew one hundred dollars to her was like fifty cents to me; she didn't need it. It was probably one of the most inconsiderate things I have experienced in a long time, and it led to my policy concerning airport transportation after that. When I go on a trip, I find a nearby lot with a shuttle to the airport and use that service. When I arrive, my car will be there and no one will be inconvenienced. If someone needs a pickup from the airport, I say, "Call me when you have left the plane and are on the way to pick up your luggage." At that point I will be on the way to pick you up.

What I did for this trip was to look in the phone book for the variety of parking areas near Nashville airport. I found one that would garage your car and provide shuttle service to and from the airport for eight dollars per day. When you look at the whole picture, you see it is well worth the cost, and no one is taken advantage of.

The Trip Begins!

The great day—Sunday July 8, 2012—had finally arrived. I left my house in suburban Nashville, Tennessee, for what could be the trip of a lifetime or a complete disappointment. I usually travel early in the day, so this trip was a departure from my usual routine of travel. I reasoned by leaving in the early evening from Nashville, I would arrive in Bergen, Norway, in the early evening, completing the greater portion of my trip. I drove to the executive park and ride and checked my car in. I was given a stub with a phone number on it and instructed to phone for pickup after my return flight the following Saturday. I loaded my bags into the shuttle bus and was dropped off at the Nashville International Airport, which was five minutes away.

At the airport I searched for the British Airways counter. After several minutes of wandering around, I discovered the Nashville-Chicago leg of the journey was going to be with American Airlines. I went to their counter, checked in one of my bags although it could have fit in overhead (later to prove to be a bad choice), and then proceeded through security. I have made it a habit to wear slip-on loafer-style shoes at least for the airport portion of my travels. I usually have enough to worry about with the laptop and the toiletries in the carry-on without having to try to lace up shoes or boots under the icy stares of the people waiting behind me. The temperature as I was leaving Nashville was 104 degrees, so perhaps some icy stares would have been welcome. I debated about wearing sandals for comfort, but I didn't think they would be appropriate on the airliner.

So after the usual and customary wait we boarded the plane for Chicago. I did notice black clouds in the distance that were approaching, and I hoped we could clear before they hit. Since I had begun to live in Nashville five years before, I had become accustomed to what appear to be hit-and-run thunderstorms. They appear to be small and to cover a small area, but they can be very robust with lightning and strong showers. Sure enough, shortly after we began the takeoff process, the pilot announced we were going to have to take a roundabout route to avoid the storms, and our arrival in Chicago would be delayed. And the anxiety began. Would another flight be available if I missed my British Airways flight scheduled for 8:35 p.m.?

We were scheduled to arrive at 7:15 p.m., so I felt we should be on time . . . but then again, I am not a pilot! So we proceeded to Chicago and went through a couple rough spots of weather on the way. The fellow sitting next to me said he too was going from Chicago to London, but he was traveling on an American Airlines flight leaving Chicago at 9:05p.m. This news made me feel a little more assured I would be able to catch a flight with American if I missed the British flight. I certainly did not want to wait until the next day if I missed the flight and have to catch a room at a local motel. Plus, it would blow up my trip schedule.

As I was watching my wristwatch, we landed in Chicago at approximately 8:15 p.m. I was beginning to get a sinking feeling as it seemed like it was taking forever to move through the line and exit the plane. On my way past the American Airlines service desk, I explained to the attendant I was going to catch a connecting flight on British Airways and wanted verification my checked-in bag would follow me. She assured me it would be on the British Airways flight. Then came the bad news. I inquired for directions to the British Airways gate and heard the dreaded phrase, "After you get on the tram." I knew upon hearing those words I was doomed. But I cowboyed up and grabbed my carry-on and laptop and began to sprint to the tram. On the tram I received more news: the gate was on the other side of the airport and the farthest point away from me.

I exited the tram and began to sprint to the British Airways desk just in time to see the plane destined for London, United Kingdom, begin to taxi away from the gate.

I identified myself to the two ladies working the desk, and one stated, "Yes, we did call for you," to which I replied, "I guess I was too busy trying to do the three-k run from the other side of the airport to hear you."

And I must admit I did work up a sweat during all that, but I am proud to report my deodorant had me covered. So after our initial exchange of pleasantries, they determined that if I wanted to travel to London, I had to be back at the American Airlines counter within twenty minutes before that flight took off. I thanked them for their efforts and after that short breather began the run back. It did seem easier this time, knowing the route, and as I made it to the desk, one of the ladies inquired, "Mr. Hahnke?" When I nodded, she motioned to the plane entrance and informed me I was the last one to board. They closed the door behind me on the plane and started with the announcement of the takeoff procedures.

In the meantime I found my seat, stashed my overhead bag, and sat back to finally relax. I just got settled and realized my golf shirt was a little bit soaked with sweat. Maybe more than a little bit. Then I suddenly smelled the unmistakable scent of BO. I was thinking, *What do I do?* I could keep my arms tucked close against my body and figure out something. Could I get into my carry-on and get to the restroom and give myself a spritz of deodorant so I didn't gross out everyone around me? I felt like I was Larry David and this trip was going to be a George Costanza disaster. I was on the aisle, and a young couple was directly on my left, and three or four people were to the left of them. Suddenly the lady next to me turned and said something to me, and I realized I was not Mr. BO. In conversation I found out she and her husband were from a part of Europe where people didn't believe in the benefits of deodorant. Suddenly I felt relieved and at ease; the Gillette had worked as it usually does.

I had brought along my Dell Mini 9 laptop for the trip instead of a full-size laptop. I felt it would be easier to work with and save some space. I played about fifty games of solitaire between Chicago and Heathrow Airport on it. I also enjoyed the little video screen they had with the programming available in the seat backs. There was the choice of drama, comedy, news, and a selection of recent movies. They offered a couple episodes of CBS *Hawaii Five-O*, which I normally enjoy, so I watched those to help pass the time. The food offered was surprisingly good. It was a chicken dish with rice and salad. And before we landed, they offered coffee and pastries. One of the items I enjoyed during the trip was the GPS-style tracker screen you could bring up on your video monitor. It displayed where you were in relation to the nearest cities and reported the number of miles/kilometers traveled and the number yet to go.

I also managed to catch a couple catnaps during the flight, so when I arrived in London, I was relatively fresh.

We arrived at approximately 11:00 a.m. London time in Heathrow Airport. Considering my British Airways flight was leaving at 2:25 p.m., we had arrived with plenty of time to spare. I didn't want a reoccurrence of the Chicago airport fiasco, now or at any other time during the trip. So bearing that in mind, I began to consider the checked-in bag situation. The checked-in bag was the one with the hiking boots, sweatshirts, heavy socks, hats, and heavy pants. It also contained the power kit for my laptop. Since I found out my laptop would not charge without the proper connector for the electricity, I had purchased a 220 to 110 transformer like we use in the United States. I also had to purchase a plug adapter because the wall outlets are different. There was also another pair of walking shoes in that bag and my shaving gear and sonic toothbrush. So I inquired about the bag at the American Airlines counter after we exited the plane. They told me British Airways would have it and it would get to my final destination.

For some reason I expected her to glance over to the lady next to her and both of them to break out laughing hysterically.

I headed over to the British Airways counter and checked in for the 2:25 p.m. flight to Bergen, Norway. While checking in I inquired about my check-in bag, as for some reason that was on my mind. The lady told me not to worry—it would arrive at my final destination. At this point after years of public service, I had to choose my words carefully. I felt like the person who had just reported a stolen car and asked when we (the police) were going to get it back. We always responded in general terms. "Soon," "They usually show up within a couple days," or "It will be very soon." I recall only one person pressing me after one of those responses, stating he needed to know exactly when we were going to locate his car. I responded, "Sometime between thirty seconds from now and never." He seemed a little astounded with my response, but about five minutes later we found out the car had been repossessed, so he knew where it was then.

Bearing that in mind I responded okay and knew I was most likely screwed in the checked bag department. I went by the duty-free area and saw they had beer as a duty-free item. I should have taken a tutorial in the duty-free part of life, and before I take another international trip, I will.

I was always confused with the meaning of *duty free*. If you buy a bottle of liquor, do you have to drink the whole thing while you are in the next country? I saw they were offering perfume and after shave; do you have to use the whole bottle during your trip? So I let it pass, which was a missed opportunity I regretted twenty-four hours later.

On the upside the flight left on time and was pleasant to Bergen. The flight was primarily over water, and the day was clear and beautiful, giving a perfect picture of the Norwegian coast and the boats along it. We had sandwiches and liquid refreshment along the way, and it was a nice short flight. After we landed I found Norway was one of the countries with duty free on arrival available. Once again I passed and went through customs and waited for my checked bag. As I stood there watching the bags come onto the carousel and the sixty or so people from my flight pick up their bags and leave, I realized I was going to be standing there alone soon with no bag.

And certainly that did happen. So I proceeded to customs, and they sent me to the airline baggage claim office. They took my information and told me that when my bag showed up, they would send it to the hotel in Odda. I did not bother to ask when, just nodded in good faith and took my copy of their report.

At times things go as planned, and I was due for that to happen. On the upside the airport is less than two hundred yards from the Bergen Clarion Hotel. I made the reservation there because I knew by this time in my trip I would be ready for a rest before the last portion of the journey. The Clarion brand is a part of the Choice Hotels chain, and I know there I will be assured of a clean top-of-the-line room. On my walk to the Clarion one of my questions about Norway was answered: they drive on the right side of the road as we do in the United States. That question was a big issue in determining if I would rent a car or take a bus for the final part of my journey.

As I approached the hotel, I noticed it was very modern appearing and the outside was spotlessly clean. I went in and checked in with desk manager Monica. She was very helpful, and I inquired if anyone was available to translate a document I had with me from Norwegian to English. She volunteered to translate during her next break in thirty minutes. I went up to my room and was delighted with its cleanliness and style.

They had a unique feature I had never come across before: the room key had to be in a slot near the front door for the lights and TV to work. It really was a good energy-saving device, as most people probably forget to shut off the lights in a motel room when leaving temporarily. There was a view overlooking the airport, and I could see Bergen in the near distance.

I went to meet with Monica at the hotel dining room/lounge. The item I needed translated was from a blog by Per A. Holst, a Norwegian author, and even with my limited knowledge of the Norwegian language I could see the blog concerned Gustav von Hahnke. Monica translated the blog and revealed it was about the accident. There were five witnesses to the event that day: another naval officer, two girls selling wild strawberries, and two teenage boys who also observed the accident from the other side of the rapids.

This was great news for my investigation—there were documented witnesses to the event, and they had been identified and interviewed.

I was hoping when I arrived in Odda I would be able to locate and possibly meet with Per A. Holst and pick up additional information.

In the meantime I mentioned my missing luggage with the charging device to Monica, and she was kind enough to come up with a spare she had and loaned it to me for a recharge. Monica, like most others in Norway, spoke English very well. I did not use my translator at all during the entire trip. I inquired with Monica about the advantages of the bus for the trip to Odda. She highly recommended the bus and told me the bus in front of the airport traveled to the main terminal every twenty minutes. She also indicated the bus drivers were very helpful and would answer questions for me. I offered to buy her dinner or give her some money to buy a treat for being so helpful to me, but she refused.

I didn't really feel like eating dinner, although the Clarion had an attractive restaurant on the main floor. I recalled a snack bar-type of bistro in the main lobby of the airport and walked over there for a sandwich and beer. While crossing over I stopped and spoke with one of the bus drivers parked in front of the airport. He relayed the fare to Odda was sixty US dollars and a couple buses arrived there and returned to Bergen several times per day. The bus appeared to be almost brand-new, and the seats looked more comfortable and had more leg room than the airline seats. It was settled: I was going to be on the bus the next morning. A rental car with all of the paperwork and insurance questions looked like a very unattractive option at this point. I went into the airport and had a light dish at the bistro there. They featured Italian food, and I had a pasta dish and a cold beer. I really did not pay attention to the prices, partially from weariness of the trip and the excitement of traveling so far.

I spent a restful night at the Clarion and woke up the next day ready to go. I went to the lobby restaurant for the complimentary breakfast. The breakfast was Norwegian style—primarily sliced meats, sliced cheese, and breads and juices. Of course fish was also available, but considering the lengthy bus trip I was preparing for, I passed on the fish. I checked out of the Clarion and went down to the airport for the bus trip. The bus was waiting at the appointed time as promised, and the driver was extremely nice and conversed with me, answering all of my questions about my route for the day. I took the local bus to the terminal and picked up a schedule there. There was no ticket office at the terminal, which made me a little apprehensive, but the driver assured me I could buy the ticket directly from the driver of my bus. The day was dark, rainy, and gloomy. The bus terminal was a ground-floor open area under an office-type building. With the gloominess it reminded me of the scenes you see in the old movies of a New York neighborhood. I was waiting to see if some guys were going to come from around the corner in leather jackets snapping their fingers.

I had missed the bus to Odda by about fifteen minutes, so I had to wait ninety minutes for the next one. I did go to some nearby shops to see what they had to offer. There was a liquor store nearby, but they didn't have Canadian Club, so I passed that by. I went back and patiently waited for the Odda bus to appear. The bus pulled up, and I was one of several getting on. The bus was spotless on the inside, and it looked like it would be a comfortable four-hour ride. The bus company was Flybussen; they certainly provided good service. We started from the terminal, and I quickly noticed it was not a nonstop trip. We stopped numerous times along the way picking up and discharging passengers. It was much like a local bus that was long-distance. It wasn't long before I realized I had made a wise choice to take the bus instead of renting a car. Once we left the urban area, the roads were a little dicey. Many spots near the mountains the roads were reduced to one lane, and if someone came from the opposite direction, one or the other had to back up. Then we approached the dock on a large lake. I assumed we were picking up passengers, but it turned out we took a ferryboat to cross the lake.

I was snapping pictures along the way, of many waterfalls and the mountains, which were still covered with ice and snow even though it was the middle of summer. There were houses with grass growing on the entire roof! It was an extremely scenic ride for the four hours and not boring at all. Finally I arrived in Odda. We stopped at the bus station in downtown, and I told the driver I was staying at the Vasstun. He assured me there was a stop immediately in front of the Vasstun and he would drop me off there. He was right on the money; he dropped me off right in front of the Hotel Vasstun. I walked across the street and went into the lobby. I was greeted by the owner and conveyed I had made Internet reservations.

She showed me to my room, which overlooked the lake directly in front of the hotel. The lake appeared to be formed from the numerous waterfalls feeding it from the melting glaciers. The room itself was nice; it was nothing fancy by any means, but considering it was an inn in a slightly remote location, I thought it was great! I had picked this inn because it was located on Route 13 almost exactly five kilometers north of the Von Hahnke memorial. I learned a long time ago if you are in a foreign country to try to make the trip as straight-line and uncomplicated as possible. It was a straight-line trip to the memorial from the hotel according to MapQuest, so I knew I was set.

It was early in the afternoon when I arrived, and I wanted to stretch my legs after two days of traveling, so I asked our hostess if it was a difficult walk to downtown Odda from the hotel or if I should consider a cab. She assured me it is all downhill and an easy walk. I walked downtown, which must have been three to five kilometers away and an easy walk, as it was all downhill. There were businesses typical of a small town and many houses. I picked up some supplemental clothing and began the trip back up. About halfway up, I decided it might be a good time to watch for a cab. Instead I saw a bus, and I was near the bus stop, so I hopped aboard. It was eight cents US to get back to the hotel. When I arrived back at the hotel, it was a good time for dinner, so I proceeded to the bar for a pre-dinner beer. I had a draft beer at the bar, which came to twenty dollars US. I was not totally surprised at the expense, as I had been forewarned by reading travel blogs. I went to the dining room for dinner; a grilled chicken breast, a scoop of steamed rice, and mixed steamed vegetables were in the vicinity of seventy dollars US. The food was delicious and moderately priced for the area. I was planning on a big day, as the next day was July 11, the 115th anniversary of the accident claiming Gustav von Hahnke.

I had to get down to see the memorial stone and get a picture next to it. I went to sleep early so I would be well rested for the excitement of the next day. Also, I wanted to be sure to get up in time to take advantage of the free breakfast included with the room.

I awoke and was startled, as I had slept late; it looked like about 11 a.m. from what I could see out my window. I had hoped I could get a quick shower in to look presentable and still be in time for breakfast. I looked at my wristwatch, and it was 1:15 a.m. It was then that it dawned on me: up near the glaciers at night, it looks like a cloudy day back home. I had a hard time falling asleep again, but eventually I did. In the morning I awoke, and after showering and cleaning up I went down for breakfast. They had sliced ham, roast beef, and a variety of sliced cheeses. They also had the best fresh-baked whole-grain bread! I had a hearty breakfast and began to plot my day.

I had planned from the start I would seek out the local police chief, identify myself to him, and ask him to direct me to a local newspaper or source for information stored locally about the incident involving Von Hahnke. Next, I would have to get up to the little memorial stone and get a picture on this anniversary date. I also planned to measure the water velocity and temperature in the rapids area. And I wanted to measure the grade of the road leading to the site and try to find any pre-1900 pictures of the road and its contours. So I called a cab and asked to be taken to the local police station. The cab driver inquired why I was going to the police station, and I gave him a condensed version of my mission. He said a local historian had done extensive research into the Von Hahnke incident, but the name escaped him. At the police station I met Sheriff Oyvind Rosseland and explained my mission. The cab driver entered the station and reported he remembered the name of the local researcher: Jan Gravdal of Odda.

A Chance Meeting

Sheriff Rosseland looked up the phone number for Jan and called him, telling him of my visit. Sheriff Rosseland related to me Jan could speak with me now if I wanted to visit his home. Of course I agreed, and the sheriff volunteered to drive me to Jan's house. On the way to Jan's house Sheriff Rosseland and I discussed the differences in law enforcement between the United States and Norway. He carried no gun, and I noticed there was no jail anywhere in town. He said the next nearest officer was halfway between Odda and Bergen, a two-hour drive. I guessed there was very little crime in the area!

Sheriff Rosseland introduced me to Jan Gravdal, his wife, and his daughter, Marie. The sheriff went on his way, and I spoke at length with Jan. He had written several works concerning the Von Hahnke tragedy and was a wealth of information. Not only did he discuss the Von Hahnke affair, but he also was able to relay some of the rich history of Odda. It appeared Odda was known as one of the stops for the rich and famous of the nineteenth century. Just prior to World War I the city invested strongly in hydroelectric power, and industry followed. At the time of my visit they enjoyed a 3 percent unemployment rate !

Jan was one of those people I could sit around and chat with for days on end. He was so knowledgeable about everything in the area and was very well spoken. I discovered he was the author of several books, which was no surprise. He gave me two books as a gift while I was there: *The Accident of Gustav von Hahnke 1897: The True Story from Odda* and *Den andre harding."* Jan had authored several others, including *Kvit Terror"*, *Den forste harding*, *Lindstrom*, and *Tyssefaldene-Krafttak I 100 ar.* The first book chronicled the events surrounding the accident at Odda. Jan was able to access some local newspaper articles not available on the Internet that gave a complete view of the incident as it was seen in 1897. The second book had a few pages regarding the Von Hahnke incident, but of the greatest interest to me was a photo from Knud Knudsen showing the rapids and the adjacent roadway where von Hahnke fell in. The photo was taken in 1898, and I had several first impressions. The road was extremely narrow; based upon the comparative size of the individual in the photo and the roadway I would estimate the road was eight to ten feet wide (2.43

to 3 meters). It would have been enough for one carriage or wagon to pass, but certainly not two. Also, there were wheel tracks in the road with one-and-one-half-foot (.304 meters) clearance on either side. On one side of the road was a sheer mountain wall; on the other were assorted pieces of rock irregularly set to form some sort of barrier from the rapids. It also appeared to be an extremely short drop from the rocks to the rapids. And last, the rapids were white from the high-velocity motion of the water. I would take all of this into account when I formed my opinion of what exactly transpired.

Jan Gravdal also mentioned there were five witnesses to the accident of Von Hahnke. At this I added I had seen a blog in Norwegian the previous February mentioning the tragedy and the witnesses by a fellow named Per A. Holst. Jan and Marie chuckled; that apparently was Jan's pen name on the blog, the blog I printed and carried along with me and had translated by Monica at the Clarion in Bergen.

Jan asked if I had been out to see the memorial yet. I replied I intended to before the day was over, as it was the 115th anniversary of the incident. He volunteered Marie to drive me there to see the memorial. I had my camera, so I was all set to go, and we drove to the site.

From all of the pictures I had seen of the memorial, I expected it to be the size of the event markers in Tennessee, probably two feet wide and three feet tall. When we approached the site, I was truly speechless (which is very rare!). There was a large parking area for twenty-plus cars, a souvenir shop directly across the road, and a large memorial. The memorial is at least ten feet tall and twelve feet wide. Tourist buses were stopped there, and people were lined up to get their pictures taken in front of the memorial. The parking lot was full, and we had to wait for a space to open. I noticed most of the cars were plated from Germany. The twin waterfalls were next to the monument, and the spray of the water immediately next to the monument had many wearing raincoats. I went to the souvenir shop across the road and saw they had a variety of Von Hahnke products. At that moment any thought I had about this being a wasted trip were long gone. I felt like I just found out I hit the lottery! All the stories my father had told me suddenly were validated! I am sure I must have looked astounded and partially in a daze; it was beyond my wildest dreams. If I had only that moment to take from the trip, it made it all worth it.

After we had taken several pictures, we had to leave because Marie had some appointments, and she dropped me off at the Hotel Vasstun.

After freshening up I decided to take a walk downtown and collect my thoughts and plot out the rest of my trip.

I determined the next day I would measure the average road grade from the downtown area to the Vasstun. After the Vasstun the upward road grade levels considerably and even goes to the other extreme of a downgrade. I also wanted to measure the speed of the rapids in the vicinity of the accident and the water temperature. These facts would come into play with my analysis of the accident and the physical condition of the victim. I had brought along a torpedo level and needed to pick up a couple other items at the local hardware store. I went to the Odda version of Ace Hardware to buy my necessary supplies. I picked up a water thermometer with a float, twenty meters of waterproof twine, a couple of balloons, a tape measure, and a Sharpie marker. Now I was set to do some measuring and come up with some opinions and theories on the accident. I returned to the hotel for a good night's rest after dinner in their dining room. I found the dinners were excellent, and I began to look forward to them every evening. A great number of locals came to enjoy dinner at the Vasstun, and such popularity is always a good seal of approval for the quality of the food.

The next morning I awoke ready to begin the final tasks of my mission—to measure the variants involved in the accident scene and begin to form my conclusions. I went down for breakfast, and the inn owner approached me with the telephone and said I had a call from the local press. I spoke with a reporter for the local newspaper, *Hardanger Folkeblad*, and he said he would like to visit with me and get the story of my mission and some pictures near the monument.

Thirty minutes later Swen Knutsen met me at the hotel lobby. He explained my visit had become local knowledge, and he wanted to do a story with some pictures. As we were going up to the memorial, I relayed a condensed version of my mission and my actions so far. Sven snapped a number of pictures and also took me to another location to show me the glaciers and their effect on the area. Sven was a wealth of information on the locality and its background. He took me to the newspaper office and introduced me to the staff. After the tour he dropped me back at the Vasstun. It was Thursday, and I had one full day left before I began my return trip. I decided to take a break and relax the remainder of the day and do my measurements on Friday.

I took a stroll downtown to take in the scenery and get a little exercise. The walk itself is scenic. The way to town is mostly along a rapid river snapping along with thousands of gallons of water at high speed. In town I stopped near the docks where the royal ships used to dock for their holiday trips. A vendor was selling freshly picked cherries, a local fruit. I bought a quart and made a snack of them on the walk back to the hotel. After dinner I decided to watch TV for a while. There were only three channels, and the programming was about song festivals and sporting events. I went to the lobby/bar, as I recalled they had a little more extensive programming. The content was basically the same but just with a larger number of channels. They did have *Two and a Half Men* and a couple other comedies, but nothing with any violence. That's when it struck me perhaps that was one of the reasons the crime rate was so low. They were not subjected to the constant stream of violence-based programming. After watching a show explaining how to cook salmon, I headed for my room and called it a night.

On Friday as I ate breakfast, I pondered about it being my last full day in Norway and decided I had to make the best of it. I also had to complete collecting my data so I could come up with my conclusions on the accident. It was another beautiful day, with the highs in the sixties (F), and I had to get first things done first. I called for a cab and had him take me up to the area of the accident. The accident actually happened two hundred to three hundred yards before the location of the memorial. The memorial had been moved from its initial location when the roads were improved in the early 1900. The large piece of granite holding the memorial plaque was actually a piece of the side of the mountain. When they moved it, they cut around the plaque and took the large piece of granite with the plaque and reset it in the parking area next to the waterfalls. There was a small bridge near the location of the accident, and I used that as a platform for most of my work.

Off the side of the bridge I lowered the thermometer into the rushing water and made several readings. It consistently read the water temperature was 43 degrees (F) (6.1 C). Next I inflated a balloon and observed it as it paced the speed of the cars northbound. The cars were traveling at approximately 40 mph (58 kph). This seemed consistent with the appearance of the water, steady white because of the velocity.

These readings were obtained 115 years to the day after the accident happened, and the conditions should have been similar then. Next I had the cab take me back to the Hotel Vasstun. Next to the hotel the rapids were flowing from the falls. I found a spot along the bank and used the thermometer again. I came up with a constant temperature of 44 degrees (F) (6.66 C). Next it was necessary to measure the grade of the road going south from the Odda port to the site of the memorial. Beyond the exercise factor I had walked from the hotel to downtown and back almost every day to become familiar with the characteristics of the road. On my walks I had observed cyclists going in both directions. The northbound cyclists were doing so with ease, as it was a downhill ride with little effort involved on their part. The southbound cyclists were usually struggling; I was walking and making better time than they were on bicycles with gears and many speeds. I recall several loudly huffing and puffing before they dismounted and walked their cycles. I went to several spots I had predetermined during my walks and measured a level line one hundred inches long. At the highest part of the one-hundred-inch line I would measure the distance to determine the grade. It fell almost consistently between six and seven inches higher than the low end. So we were dealing with a 6 to 7 percent grade from the docks to the area of the Hotal Vasstun, where the road began to level off and possibly begin a slight downhill slope toward the waterfalls. I then used MapQuest to determine the distance between the dock and the Hotel Vasstun. It indicated a distance of 1.7 miles, or 2.73 kilometers, for that portion of the trip. I used the same method to determine the distance between Vasstun and the memorial, and I came up with 3.29 miles, or 5.29 kilometers.

I felt at this point I had accomplished what I had come for and went back to the hotel and began to pack. My long-lost bag had arrived a couple days before, so I now had the complete set to prepare for transport the next morning. I made a quick trip downtown to pick up a copy of the latest *Folkeblad*, with a full-page story of the visit of Robert von Hahnke to the memorial and my mission. It is also online at http://www.hardanger-folkeblad.no/hfnyhende/article6147777.ece.

Three buses were leaving Odda for Bergen in the morning. One was at approximately 6 a.m. (forget that), another was at 9 a.m., and the

other was at 11 a.m. Although my scheduled flight did not leave Bergen until 6:20 p.m., I chose to take the 9 a.m. In the event of a problem on the way, I could always have the 11 a.m. bus as a backup. Watching my plane depart without me once on the trip was more than enough.

I was up early the next morning and enjoyed the last breakfast at the Hotel Vasstun. Although the scenery was terrific and the people I met were great, it was time to get back home. After breakfast I settled my tab and bid farewell to all, taking a cab to the Odda bus station. There was a bus stop right in front of the hotel, but I could picture the driver not seeing me and driving by to Odda. I knew he had to stop at Odda, so that was a sure bet.

The cab stand was about fifty yards away from the bus station, so it was an easy ride. Incidentally, it seems like English is a very acceptable second language for everyone in Norway. As I mentioned earlier, I did not have to use my translator once during the whole trip.

So there I was at the bus station about thirty minutes early, and I reached into my pocket, and of course I had the key to my room at the Vasstun. I had a gut feeling these inns did not have a lot of keys floating around. I didn't want to leave the bus station, as my bus had pulled in and the driver was taking a break before we headed out. What would happen if I grabbed a cab to go back to the Vasstun and it broke down on the trip or got into an accident? Would I have the cab chasing down the bus because I was late?

It was a one hundred Kroner (twenty dollars US) to get from the inn to the bus station. I hustled over to the cab stand, saw my driver, and gave him one hundred kroner and the key, asking him to deliver it to the inn the next time he was up that way today. So that potential emergency was settled.

When the driver returned from his break, I loaded up my bags and paid my sixty-dollar fare before settling back to enjoy the ride. I was going to take the opportunity to snooze, but the scenery was too tempting, so I enjoyed it on the way to Bergen. We took a different route from the one used earlier, and this time we took two ferries to cross two large lakes. My anxiety started to kick in, as I started to think, *This had better be going to Bergen, or I don't know what I am going to do!* We continued on, and at one stop a woman passenger got on and helped me solve a mystery that had been bugging me for a couple years.

I found out it was not because of George Bush that Europeans disliked Americans! It was not because of Barack Obama that Europeans disliked Americans! It was because of Americans like the one on the bus that Europeans disliked Americans. This woman got on the bus smelling like she had been dipped in perfume ten minutes before boarding the bus. Did she think she had to finish the bottle from the duty-free before returning? She commenced to get into a conversation with the lady beside her (that poor thing must have regretted knowing English as a second language at this point!) and of course, she spoke loudly enough for three quarters of riders to clearly hear the conversation. I was fully in my Norwegian mode; I have very European features, and I was clutching on to my edition of the *Hardanger* Folkeblad, so as long as I didn't open my mouth, I blended in as one of the locals.

The woman went on to introduce herself to the lady next to her, saying that she was a professor of art at a university in the Midwest and had come to Norway to explore some of the artistic outlets there. I noticed a lot of rolling eyes from the passengers in seats around her. She went on to pontificate about her staff at the school and how important she was. The lady next to her, with a few questions, solicited responses indicating the woman was an instructor at a junior college. And that junior college had no academic prerequisites for entry; just come up with the tuition, and you were in! Many of the passengers surrounding the woman looked like they were about to burst into laughter. I found it humorous and at the same time sad. What steps do you have to take in trying to impress people you have never seen before and will most likely never see again?

I bookmarked her face and vowed not to sit next to her on the eight-hour flight from London to New York.

Arriving in Bergen with plenty of time to spare, I went to the Bergen Airport Clarion and looked for Monica to return her computer charging cord (European version). She was not in, so I left her a note thanking her for all of her help with the cord and a copy of the *Folkeblad*. I grabbed another Italian meal at the airport and went through security for the flight. This time I went to the duty-free shop and made a couple purchases. My flight plan had me landing in London at Heathrow Airport at 7:30 p.m. on Saturday night. The flight from Heathrow to JFK in New York was leaving Heathrow at 10:45 a.m. the next morning. I reserved a room at the Choice Hotels Comfort Hotel near the airport. Knowing this stopover would give me a chance to consume any duty-free consumables I picked up, I got a six-pack of Carlsberg beer and two packs of twenty-four Mars bar miniatures. I was going to get only one pack of the Mars bars, but the girl at the counter insisted I had to buy two because they had a tag on them two for so many dollars. I told her I didn't want two; I only wanted one no matter the price. So she rang me up at the special price for two and put two in the bag, stating, "Here is your candy." I hesitated for a second and then said, "Thank you." I could have argued, but perhaps it was the local custom. I was just happy I avoided any real specials of ten-for.

I Love New York (Maybe a Little)

So I boarded the plane without incident, and we were off for the one-hour flight (time zones) to London Heathrow. The flight was enjoyable; they served a little meal, and it was a smooth flight. After we landed at Heathrow, I collected my bags and jumped into a cab that took me to the Quality Inn. As I was checking in, they mentioned a dinner special they were featuring at the in-house restaurant, and I opted for that.

After checking into my room I headed to the restaurant. The food was exceptional: a stuffed mushroom cap, roast beef, vegetables, and dessert. I retired to my room to relax with some TV and the six-pack of Carlsberg. Two beers were it for me, and I hit the hay, setting the alarm for 7 a.m.

Sunday morning I awoke feeling refreshed and looking forward to completing my trip. I showered and cleaned up, packed my bags, and was ready to head to the airport. I phoned the front desk to call a cab for me, and they informed me they had a shuttle running to the airport in fifteen minutes, so I opted for that. The shuttle ride to the airport was comfortable, and things were running smoothly on the trip so far.

Checking in involved going through security again. I had several little motel-type shampoo containers in my carry-on; they had been with me from the start of the trip. Suddenly there was a big frenzy at Heathrow; those shampoo containers were contraband! The little security guy was nice about it, saying they would be checked and if they were found not to contain anything offensive, I could have them back. I told him not to bother, as I was going to be home in my own shower with my own shampoo before the day was done. He would hear nothing of it; I was ordered to stand by while he checked them out. He returned a moment later with the shampoos in a zipper lock bag proclaiming they were okay to transport. The next victim was my little bottle of roll-on deodorant. I just knew the deodorant would get it! I had bought the roll-on in Odda for the return trip because I packed my toiletries in my checked bag. So the deodorant went through the process and made it to the plane.

Boarding the plane went well until I was seated. I am a fairly tall guy, and usually the crew helps me out by putting me in an aisle seat at the front so I can get some leg room. This time I had the aisle seat, but it was behind some schmo who put his seat back immediately as far as it would go. I felt like he was resting on my knees. It also made it next to impossible to use the video screen unless I wanted to arrive in New York looking like the hunchback of Notre Dame. Of course they showed a promo film about how the airline was expanding seat room to make flying more comfortable in the future. If I made it through this flight, I surely would enjoy some decent room in future flights! The guy in front of me made the mistake of getting up to use the restroom after we took off.

I used the opportunity to press his seat bottom and return it to the upright position. When he returned, I had my knees braced forward so he could recline only so far. This tactic gave me a little more room, and I could even enjoy the video monitor. The flight back was similar to the flight over—long but a little entertaining. The same films I had viewed on the video monitor on the way over seemed a little better on the way back.

Finally I arrived in New York! It was 1:30 p.m., and my flight to Nashville left at 5:00 p.m. With plenty of time I had to go through US customs and security again. Beyond the super-long lines, that all went well. I checked my one bag again and was tempted to check the carry-on bag just so I didn't have to lug it around, but at the last moment I decided not to check it. That turned out to be a good choice. So while I was in New York at JFK, I had to get a corned beef sandwich on an onion roll. One can't go through New York without a corned beef on onion roll unless there are extreme circumstances. While wandering through the airport I come across Brooklyn National Deli, the perfect spot for a corned beef on onion roll. It's like when you travel to Detroit, you can't drive past American Coney Island without stopping in for a couple dogs with everything! So I got in line, and in a couple minutes I had my corned beef on an onion roll with a Diet Coke, headed for the gate for the final leg of my journey. I checked in and plopped down in a seat and began to wolf down the sandwich. In less than four hours I was going to be home. I would call the Executive parking people from the airport, and in ten minutes I would be in my car on the Briley Parkway headed home. I had to work the next day, but the return trip was scheduled in such a way that I was rested and would be ready to go Monday morning. Finally the moment arrived: the plane was boarded, and with the time change I would be home within two hours. We taxied down to the runway and stopped short as I noticed other flights leaving and taking off. This went on and on. I could not understand why we were not in the line leaving. I timed the arrivals on the runway a little distance from us, and they were coming in like clockwork every several minutes. I noticed bigger planes than ours were leaving every several minutes as we sat there.

Finally we started to move but in the wrong way, back to the terminal. The pilot announced we were reaching the two-and-one-half-hour limit for sitting out watching everyone else leave, so the flight was canceled.

I was dumbfounded! So close! And now what happened? Everyone left the plane and went back to the service counter. The attendants told me they would reschedule me on another flight for Nashville, but it would be the next morning out of LaGuardia Airport. And it would not be a direct flight; it would be via Dallas, Texas. As the old saying goes, "It's a crappy deal, but it's the only one you have." So I grabbed my tickets for the next day and went down to get my checked luggage, and of course I could not find my checked luggage. After searching for a while I decided the most of the contents was dirty laundry; I had enough on my mind, so I was not going to worry about that bag at this point. It would show up eventually. I started to become concerned about having a room to stay for the night. I was directed to a phone bank at the exit of the airport connected to several hotel chains. I found the Choice Hotels phone and told them my plight and the need for a room. Right then one of the baggage carriers, who was standing about three feet away from me, had to start barking orders to Vinnie at the top of his lungs, although Vinnie was about ten feet away from him. I gave that guy the "if looks could kill" look, making it clear that for two cents I would have pulled that phone out of the wall and cheerfully clubbed him with it. He moved on. Sorry, buddy, but I just wasn't in the mood for your foolishness.

The people from the Choice Hotels found me a Jacuzzi suite at a hotel between JFK and LaGuardia, gave me the address, and assured me the room would be held for me. My contact with them was the one bright spot (besides the corned beef) of the whole stop there. I stepped out of the airport, computer bag in one hand and carry-on in the other, to face a line of cabs. I walked by a Crown Vic, and the drive rolled down the window and asked if I needed a cab. I responded I did and was going to the Quality Inn, and I gave him the address. He responded he knew where it was, and we put my luggage in the trunk and off we went. I noticed there was no meter in the cab and asked where it was. He said, "Don't worry; it is twenty dollars." After we passed the same intersection three times, I asked him if he was sure he knew where he was going. He asked me for the address again, and we proceeded on. He stopped at a Quality Inn, but it was not my Quality Inn. I told him to wait while I checked if it was the right one. Of course it wasn't, so I gave the driver the instructions the desk clerk had given me. We ended up driving around in circles for another forty-five minutes until I spotted a Clarion Inn. I ordered the driver to go there, gave him his twenty dollars, and yanked my bags out of the trunk. I went into the Clarion and explained my problem, and they called a "town car" they were familiar with, and he drove me to the correct location without further delay or incident.

So I checked in and inquired about a cab to LaGuardia early the next morning. They assured me I could catch a cab and get there in time for my flight. I e-mailed my boss saying I would not be at work the next day, thanks to American Airlines. I went up and relaxed in the Jacuzzi and got a good night's sleep.

I woke up early, gathered up my belongings, and headed down to the lobby at about 4:30 a.m. The desk clerk told me I was way too early, but I told him to call the cab regardless. Nothing was going to go wrong today for the flight to Tennessee. The town car picked me up and drove me to the airport without incident. It was getting crowded there even that early in the morning. It took a while to clear security, and then I grabbed a bagel and coffee at Dunkin' Donuts and relaxed before the flight. I saw a young guy from Cookeville, Tennessee, who had sat next to me on our almost flight to Nashville the day before. He said he could not find an available hotel room and had ended up sleeping on a heating grate at the airport. I was glad I had Choice Hotels looking out for me! Before long we were boarding, and off to Dallas we went. It was my first time at the

Dallas airport, and I was impressed by how clean and well laid out it was. I had a Pizza Hut lunch special and relaxed until our flight to Nashville was ready to board.

On the flight to Nashville I was sitting next to a gentleman and his wife, who were about my age. By now I was almost giddy with the feeling this trip was finally over. He made the mistake of asking about my trip, and I blurted out the story during the two-hour flight. When we arrived in Nashville, he probably was happier than I was to get off the plane!

After we were off the plane, I once again looked for the elusive checked bag. It was nowhere to be found. I went to the baggage claim office and filed a report. At this point I didn't care; there were some notes and books I needed for my research, but beyond that it was just a collection of dirty laundry.

I phoned Executive Travel and Parking and relayed my stub number, and they had a shuttle over to pick me up in minutes. When I arrived at their location, my car was running with the AC blasting and ready to go. If only the whole trip would have gone so smoothly! I was home in about thirty minutes, and it felt great to be back. The first thing I did was get into a swimsuit, grab a cold beer, and get into my Jacuzzi. The Jacuzzi in motels are okay, but there is nothing like your own, with the water temperature set just right, the water clarity as you like it, and no strangers having been in it. It's like being in your favorite bed or chair. I did double time in it to help me feel better after almost two days of continuous travel sitting in those airport or airplane chairs. It sure felt good!

CENTRAL CHANCERY OF THE ORDERS OF KNIGHTHOOD
ST JAMES'S PALACE, SW1A 1BH
TELEPHONE 020 7930 4832
FAX 020 7839 2983

From: Miss Rachel Wells, CVO

2nd November 2012

Reference: 19/5/12

Dear Mr. Von Hahnke,

I am writing to acknowledge and thank you for your letter of 28th September to the Royal Archives in connection with your late great great uncle, Field Marshal Count Wilhelm Von Hahnke, GCVO, which they have forwarded to us.

According to our records, His Excellency Field Marshal Wilhelm Von Hahnke was appointed to be an Honorary Knight Grand Cross of the Royal Victorian Order on 15th June 1907, on the occasion when he represented His Imperial Majesty, The German Emperor and King of Prussia, on the unveiling of the Statue in London of His Royal Highness The Duke of Cambridge. At that time the Field Marshal was the Governor of Berlin.

Enclosed is a copy of The London Gazette of 18th June 1907, in which the honour was announced; you will see that his ADC, Captain Ludwig von Baumbach, was made an Honorary Member of the Fourth Class of the Order on the same occasion.

Despite a search of the information available to them, I regret the Royal Archives have not been able to add any more details.

I hope the above will be of interest. As I am sure you will know, Count Von Hahnke died on 8th February 1912.

Yours sincerely,

Rachel Wells

Assistant Secretary

Mr. Robert Von Hahnke,
1404 Windhill Ct.,
Greenbrier,
TN 37073,
Tennessee,
United States of America

CHAPTER SEVEN

Now It's Down to Business

Now to put the facts together and arrive at a conclusion of what most likely happened in the Von Hahnke incident. Not only do we want to determine if the death was due to an accident, but we also want to arrive at a conclusion of why the leader of a nation would construct an elaborate memorial for a lieutenant killed in a seemingly accidental fashion. That of all things to me at first glance was the biggest mystery of the whole investigation.

We have established through documented newspaper articles of the period that Wilhelm von Hahnke was probably one of the more important people in Europe in his time. We must surmise how he rose to the position, considering the circumstances of the time.

He was fortunate to become, by several accounts, friends with Kaiser Friedrich I early during his career in the German army.

Being Prussian by birth gave him an advantage, as the Prussians were looked upon as the elite of the German military. Also, the German royalty seemed to have a preoccupation with the military and military uniforms. They must have had an extensive wardrobe of army and navy uniforms, one for every occasion. Photo records and paintings featuring the kaisers show that it was rare they were not in some kind of uniform. And it was not just the kaisers. I observed a picture with Kaiser Wilhelm II posing with cousin Czar Nicholas of Russia, each wearing the other's military uniform. Nicholas had the Picklehaube (pike helmet), and Wilhelm II was wearing the Russian cap. Nicholas was smiling; Wilhelm II didn't look so happy. But regardless, one would be hard pressed to find a picture of Wilhelm II not in some sort of a military uniform. In any event, Wilhelm von Hahnke, being good friends with Prince Friedrich before his ascension to the throne, no doubt became somewhat of an uncle figure to young Wilhelm. This relationship no doubt went on for years before

Wilhelm II was elevated to the throne. Von Hahnke no doubt was kept as an adviser, giving the kaiser a mature point of view on all subjects concerning the military and the state. The kaiser apparently knew he could trust Von Hahnke to advise him of the correct path and to represent him in any venue without worry of any deceptions. When we look upon the limited records we have of von Hahnke's travels representing the kaiser in the royal houses of Europe and the Middle East, it would be safe to assume the kaiser trusted Von Hahnke completely.

Would this relationship extend further and have Kaiser Wilhelm in the role of uncle to the Von Hahnke children? When Von Hahnke's first (Wilhelm) was born (1867), Kaiser Wilhelm was eight years old. The youngest was born in 1873 when the kaiser was fourteen years old. I think it would be very possible young Kaiser Wilhelm may have seen himself in an uncle position to the offspring of the family friend. Three of the four Von Hahnke sons went into the military and followed in their father's footsteps. I can see how this close relationship revolving around the military would foster a close relationship between the two families. Also, Von Hahnke was looked upon as one of the leaders of the group, similar to the Knights of the Round Table in medieval literature. But the roles were reversed, and the king was the young one and the knights were the seasoned warriors. It would make sense the offspring of the knights would be groomed to take their place as they moved on and the kaiser became older. Also, the loyalty would be handed down from father to son in the service of the kaiser.

So let's deal first with the newspaper rumors linking young Von Hahnke to the black eye the kaiser suffered. Several newspapers latched on to this theory of Von Hahnke's getting into a fistfight with the kaiser on board the royal yacht. Some accounts say Von Hahnke was drunk when the alleged attack happened. I have to discount that part of the story for two reasons. First, it was on a Sunday morning, and according to the story Von Hahnke was riding his bicycle on the deck of the ship. Have you ever seen a drunk ride a bicycle any distance? A short time later Von Hahnke rode the bicycle on a five-mile (eight-kilometer) trip. A great portion of that trip was up a 6 to 7 percent-grade road.

When I was taking my almost daily walks to and from downtown Odda, it was partially to study the road and the rigors of a bicycle trip. I often saw riders going uphill in their bicycles with many gears and all of the modern advantages. On some portions of the road I was making better time walking, and they were loudly panting as they pedaled. I cannot conceive of any intoxicated person getting very far on the road with that kind of grade.

The second most apparent reason is if anyone dared to strike the kaiser, they would no doubt be put in chains and whisked to the German destroyer escort that always accompanied the royal yacht. I am sure the person would be sitting in the brig in that ship until they decided what to do with him. I am certain they would not release him and tell him to go on foreign soil for a bike ride through the countryside. Also, I cannot imagine the tall, muscular Von Hahnke fighting with the smaller kaiser, whose one arm was so crippled he needed aid in dressing and cutting his food at meals. The family relationship between the kaiser and the Von Hahnkes also must be considered. Based on his father's devotion to the royal family, I find it extremely doubtful Gustav would strike the kaiser or disrespect him in any way, shape, or form.

In addition, no officers or men assigned to the royal yacht ever came forward to substantiate the "black eye by Von Hahnke" story. We are able to look back and know that if the story were to have any truth to it, one of the crew members would have stepped forward later and become the new hero to the press. Especially after the kaiser abdicated the throne in 1918, if someone was going to step forward, they could have done so without fear of repercussions if the truth was contrary to the official explanation of the tragedy. It never happened.

Next, we have the bicycle trip itself. Lieutenant von Hahnke was going with Lieutenant von Lewetzow on their time off to the "King of the Waterfalls" south of Odda on what is now Route 13. According to all reports it was a normal summer day with clear weather. I consider an important part of the investigation the ride toward the falls before the accident. The first 1.7 miles (2.73 kilometers) were on the roads with 6 to 7 percent grade. The roads may be different now, but one cannot change the angle from the docks at the center of Odda to the edge of the glacial mountains now near the Hotel Vasstun. I spoke with a local (Tennessee) expert on bicycles, Lawrence Russell of Woodbury, Tennessee, to get an insight into the bicycles of that age. He responded the bicycles of the 1890s to 1900s were notorious for poor braking. The brakes for the front wheel were the hand-grip type of today, but modern brakes pinch the metal rim of the wheel with brake pads to stop. The 1890s brake system gripped the tire instead of the rim. Also, the brake pad was normally a piece of wood. He relayed that many accidents were caused by the braking system of the older bikes. The steering mechanism was also poor compared to that of today, with no shock absorber to assist in control on a bumpy washboard type of road.

The bicycle most likely would have been aone-speed. The trip up the incline in the road leaving Odda must have been exhausting! Also bear in mind there was no safety equipment involved, with no helmet or knee or elbow pads as would be worn today. There was no hydrating devices like we have today, and Von Hahnke was in a German navy uniform that was most certainly not made for exercise. Per A. Holst reported in his blog of February 2012 that two young girls were reportedly witness to the aftermath of the accident. They were selling strawberries on what is now Route 13 when Lieutenant Lewetzow stopped to chat with them, and Von

Hahnke rode on a little farther. Apparently he moved on to catch up with Von Hahnke and observed him in the rapids, holding his bloody head and trying to fight the rapids. There were also two teenaged boys on the other side of the rapids who observed the aftermath of the accident. Von Hahnke's hat was the only thing left behind. Apparently Von Lewetzow began to attempt to aid Von Hahnke, but the others held him back, as they knew the power of the rapids.

I observed a photo of the spot in the road where Von Hahnke left it. The photo was by Knut Knutsen, a famous photographer of the era in that area. It was in a book by Jan Gravdal concerning the Von Hahnke accident. The photo showed the narrow road with some ruts made by carriages or wagons. I also noticed the edge along the river had a series of large stones arranged as a guard barrier. Upon close examination I noticed the stones were not flush, but there were sizable gaps between them. These were probably sufficient for wagons or carriages, but a bicycle could easily slip between them. Several theories have been cast about over the years that Von Hahnke went between the stones into the river. One theory was he went to wipe the sweat off his brow and lost control, dropped his hat, and went into the rapids. Another theory is he ran over some horse droppings that negated his braking system completely, and he went in. Another is that a reckless carriage forced him off the road and into the rapids. Any or all of those theories could be true, but the fact remains he ended up in the water, the rushing whitewater rapids fed by the melting glaciers and focusing their strength to that point.

Me pointing to spot where Lieutenant von Hahnke fell in (photo by Sven Knutsen of *Hardanger Folkeblad*).

I did notice that at that area of the rapids, although shallow (two to three feet), the base was loaded with jagged rocks. With water that shallow a body would certainly be driven from jagged rock to jagged rock. Once in that water, a person would not stand much of a chance unless he was pulled out immediately.

Another factor we must consider is the hypothermia effects. Taking a person immediately from a strenuous workout such as the bicycle trip on a warm summer day and then immersing that body in forty-three-degree

(F) rushing water would swiftly bring on hypothermia. Even a person of supposed athletic prowess such as Von Hahnke would be helpless in a short period of time and be at the mercy of the rapids.

Confusion, fatigue, and lack of coordination are all symptoms induced by hypothermia. It would not take long for a person in those conditions to give up the struggle and succumb to the battering water and jagged stones. At water speeds of thirty-five to forty miles per hour, it would not take long for a body to be swept away from the sight of the onlookers!

In my opinion, the condition of near fatigue in Von Hahnke as he drove his bicycle contributed to his accident. Had he stopped when Von Lewetzow did for a break, he might have been better prepared for whatever conditions caused him to lose control. Also, by continuing on, he worsened the effects of the frigid water on his body when he became immersed. Had he stopped for a few moments before, his body might have cooled down some and the effects of hypothermia might have been lessened.

It is my professional opinion that fatigue was the primary cause of the accident, because the contributing factors mentioned in the press and other sources could have been averted by a bicyclist alert and responsive to the threats. It is difficult to investigate an accident or crime even several days after, but it is even more so 115years later. Had the incident just happened, we would have been able to measure the tracks leading to the river to determine the exact direction of travel of the vehicle. We would have recovered the bicycle and given it a thorough examination of brakes, steering, suspension, tires, frame, and seating. We would have interviewed all potential witnesses and had written statements made with their point of view, and we would have elaborated on their observations. The press at the time tossed a dummy into the water several days after the accident to witness the effects. They reported the dummy figure was torn to shreds within moments. Having no knowledge of the composition of the test dummy, I find it tough to give much credibility to their study. I would not bother to do a test dummy today if I was investigating the same type of accident. In looking at the rapids, one can see it is certain a person would be dead with a couple minutes and several hundred yards of travel in the whitewater and jagged stones. No usable information would be obtained from the dummy.

So, in conclusion, we know from reported eyewitness accounts that Von Hahnke was in the water on the date and time in question. He struggled briefly and was swept away by the rapids, getting pummeled by the jagged rocks. His body was recovered at a later date much farther down the river.

Now to the next question: why the big memorial to a lieutenant in the German navy who died of an accident on a luxury cruise through the scenic summer resorts of Norway? He had a job most people in the military—or for that matter, most everyone—would love. Being an officer aboard the royal yacht would not involve much physical labor. The food had to be the greatest; escorting the kaiser when he wanted to go onshore was probably the biggest duty he had. The royal ship went all over Europe and once on a trip to the United States. All of the different ports where the ship would stop would be exciting—London, the French Riviera, and Italy, to mention a few. And considering your father was the chief of staff and your family had a close relationship with the Kaiser, it had to be one of the greatest jobs there ever was! But it also makes me wonder, did the close family friend the kaiser tell Herr and Frau von Hahnke he would keep an eye on young Gustav and no harm would come to him? He would be near the kaiser during most of these trips, and what safer place could there be? Young Von Hahnke could get some sea experience and end up moving up the ladder on fast track after his term on the royal yacht. Or could he be close to the kaiser being groomed to take over his father's post? Would he have been the kaiser's representative traveling to the royal courts of Europe and the Middle East acting as the personal spokesperson for the kaiser and the German people? All of these things were possible, and I contend very probable. Then the kaiser got injured in an accident on board the ship one morning. Von Hahnke knew the kaiser well enough to stay clear of him for a while until tempers simmered down.

The Road (Rt 13) back in early 1900

An excursion onshore with a fellow officer sightseeing would have been the perfect excuse to get away and give the kaiser time to cool down.

Then the accident happened, and worst of all, no body was immediately available. When the body was discovered almost a month later, the kaiser sent a ship to pick him up and bring him back to Berlin for burial. Gustav was buried with full military honors. One year after the accident the kaiser dedicated the monument to Lieutenant Gustav von Hahnke in Odda at the spot where he fell into the water. It was reported to be a well-attended ceremony with dignitaries from the navies of several countries attending. It was a large plaque with the Von Hahnke coat of arms and an inscription dedicating it to Gustav von Hahnke, son of Wilhelm von Hahnke, from Kaiser Wilhelm II and the officers of the royal yacht.

Knowing all (or all that is possible to know) of the facts surrounding this, I feel the kaiser was attempting to ease the suffering of the parents and family he was close to. He erected this large monument to display his affection for the family and the loss of their son. I find it ironic that many of the German memorials were destroyed during the wars in Europe, but this memorial still stands proud in Norway, away from the ravages of war. It also stands in what was a neutral nation during World War I.

I think it also represents the dedication of a fallen young navy officer's father to maintaining peace during a very turbulent time in the world. There were many small wars during that period of time, and Germany managed to stay out of them. The Boer War involved Great Britain and the Boers of South Africa. The Boers were loosely of German heritage, so Germany could have made an excuse to enter the fray on their side but didn't. There was rumor Germany may have been supplying the Boers with some arms, but that was never substantiated. There was also the Russian-Japanese war, which would have given Germany an opportunity to take advantage of a two-front war on Russia. That would have provided the golden opportunity to have the advantage over the larger Russian army, but that path was not taken. The kaiser chose to take the advice of his senior general and closest adviser, Wilhelm von Hahnke. Wilhelm von Hahnke was awarded prestigious medals from Russia and Great Britain, among others, for his peacekeeping efforts. I find it more than coincidental that within two years of General von Hahnke's death, the European countries were involved in World War I.

At this point I want to thank you for allowing me to share this trip of discovery. There were different turns in the process over the years, with everything coming to a conclusion with the trip to Norway and the discovery of the large monument and the scenic area around it. I had never had any inclination to travel to Norway prior to this investigation; I am more of a warm-country type of tourist. I have previously been to Brazil and most countries in the Caribbean region. After I retired from the state police, it was not long before I moved down south to the Virginia-North Carolina border. The first year I lived there I was still using my jet ski during the end of October, and I brought it out again in April. I now reside in Tennessee near Nashville, and the weather is very similar. I never had pictured going on a trip to a cold-weather place for any reason. While I was in Norway, Sven from the local newspaper related how the waterfalls freeze and the roads are often impassable during the winter.

So in a final analysis of the investigation and trip, we have the following facts:

General Wilhelm von Hahnke was the most trusted adviser of Kaiser Wilhelm II prior to World War I.

General von Hahnke traveled extensively representing the kaiser and the German government.

General von Hahnke was a constant companion to the kaiser and the royal family during most public appearances, both internationally and within Germany.

General von Hahnke began a relationship with the royal family starting with Kaiser Friedrich and continuing with Kaiser Wilhelm II up to Von Hahnke's death in 1912.

Discovery of an obituary from the *Neue Preubische Zeitung* July 15, 1897, published in the book *Der Unfall Des Gustav von Hahnke 1897: The Accident of Gustav von Hahnke,* by Per A. Holst, indicates General von Hahnke was married to Josphine von Bulow, and they had five sons and one daughter. The Von Bulow family had many high-ranking members in the German military, dating back to the early 1800s. Elizabeth von Schlieffen was married to General von Hahnke's eldest son, Wilhelm. I incorrectly surmised earlier that she was married to General von Hahnke, as biographical information on her is sketchy at best. When I made that incorrect assumption, I asserted that the gold standard of proof for marriages and siblings is most often the obituary notice.

The death of Gustav von Hahnke was purely accidental, and there was never any substantial evidence or credible testimony presented to the contrary.

Gustav von Hahnke was involved in a fatal bicycle accident, most likely caused by equipment malfunction or failure contributed to by operator fatigue.

The high speed, rushing, and near-frigid water Gustav von Hahnke was immersed in following the strenuous lengthy ride on the bicycle quickly would have caused hypothermia, contributing to his being overwhelmed by the rushing waters.

The water on the 115th anniversary of the fatal accident averaged two to three feet deep, and the bottom of the stream was completely covered with jagged rocks. Being pummeled against these rocks by the whitewater flow would make survival very short.

The memorial constructed under the direction of the kaiser is large and impressive. It was built in part out of the admiration the kaiser had for the family of his closest adviser, General von Hahnke. There appears to have been no other motivation for the kaiser to provide this honor to the family in a foreign land.

The memorial had initially been along the road on the mountain wall, but it was moved to its present location when the road was modernized.

It is now mounted in the southern portion of a large paved parking lot immediately before the bridge over the flow from the Twin Waterfalls. There is a souvenir and gift shop immediately across the road. While I was there several times, I observed many tourists having their pictures taken in front of the memorial. The parking lot was always busy with tour buses and private cars from as far away as Germany.

Louis Hahnke knew his family had a strong presence in the German army prior to World War I, but he did not mention and probably never knew of the Von Hahnke memorial.

The Internet provided many clues to assist in my search, but many were false and misleading. The pictures on the Internet of the memorial would lead one to believe it is probably three feet high, as there is no one standing nearby to give the picture perspective.

Field Marshal Wilhelm von Hahnke is not mentioned but rarely if at all in most writings involving the kaiser. This may be because von Hahnke was prominent during the years of the kaiser's reign in peacetime. After Von Hahnke's death it was nearly two years later that Germany found itself at war with its former friends.

When the kaiser abdicated in 1918, it was the end of the Von Hahnke dynasty in the German army. A search of the post-World War I records shows none of the von Hahnke clan involved in the military.

I discovered the Von Hahnke coat of arms on the memorial, so I now have that for my records. Prior to the trip I had no idea there was a family coat of arms.

The trip was completed with my satisfaction the truth had been uncovered. The interesting twist to my search was the fact I ended up in Norway to do the research Until the point when I discovered the memorial, I was convinced I would have to travel to Berlin, Germany, in order to do research. Because of the conditions reported by my father, I did not consider the trip to Berlin as being very promising. I knew at best I would be searching military cemeteries for evidence of the Von Hahnkes, and that could be exhausting in both time and results. The

Invalidenfriedhof Cemetery in Berlin is the last resting place for many German military of the time period in question. I attempted to find a Von Hahnke in their online burial records with no success. The big problem with the Invalidenfriedhof Cemetery is the fact the Russians during their occupation built the famous Berlin Wall through a lot of it, what happened to the graves in their path of the wall is questionable.

I wrote this book due in part to the twists and turns my journey took. As a result of the trip I changed my legal name back to the original family name of Von Hahnke just prior to the publication of this book. When I related the story to many of my friends and associates, they all agreed it would be the best thing to do.

I hope you will take my lead in this book and investigate your family background to pass on to your family. Remember, if you find something you don't like, you can keep it buried. But hopefully you will be as fortunate as I am and have a story to relate to your children and grandchildren that may give them inspiration to achieve greatness in their careers and lives.

My Mother, Mary Joan Hahnke passed away August 2009 in a Detroit area nursing home after a lengthy stay due to Alzheimer's Disease. Any savings or possessions her and my Father Lou had accumulated during their lives were used for her care during those years. I look upon it as they left the best legacy one could ever wish for, a clue, an invitation, to an adventure filled with exciting discoveries, at each turn more than I would dare wish or dream for. I ended up with an inheritance no amount of money could ever buy. Just before the completion of this work I legally changed my name back to the original European version Von Hahnke, reminding me everyday where I came from.

www.ingramcontent.com/pod-product-compliance
Lightning Source LLC
Chambersburg PA
CBHW051432280526
45785CB00003B/1261